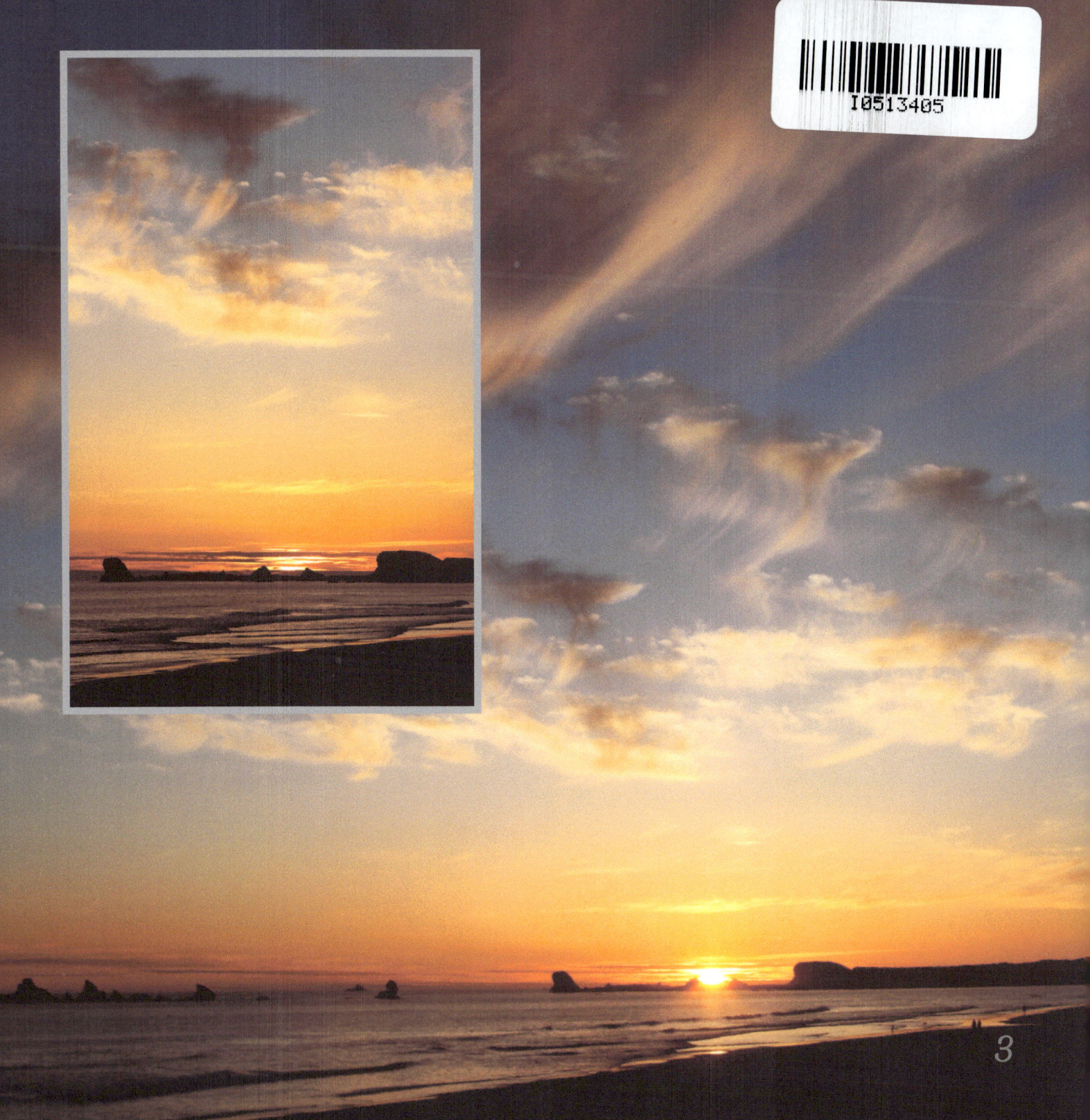

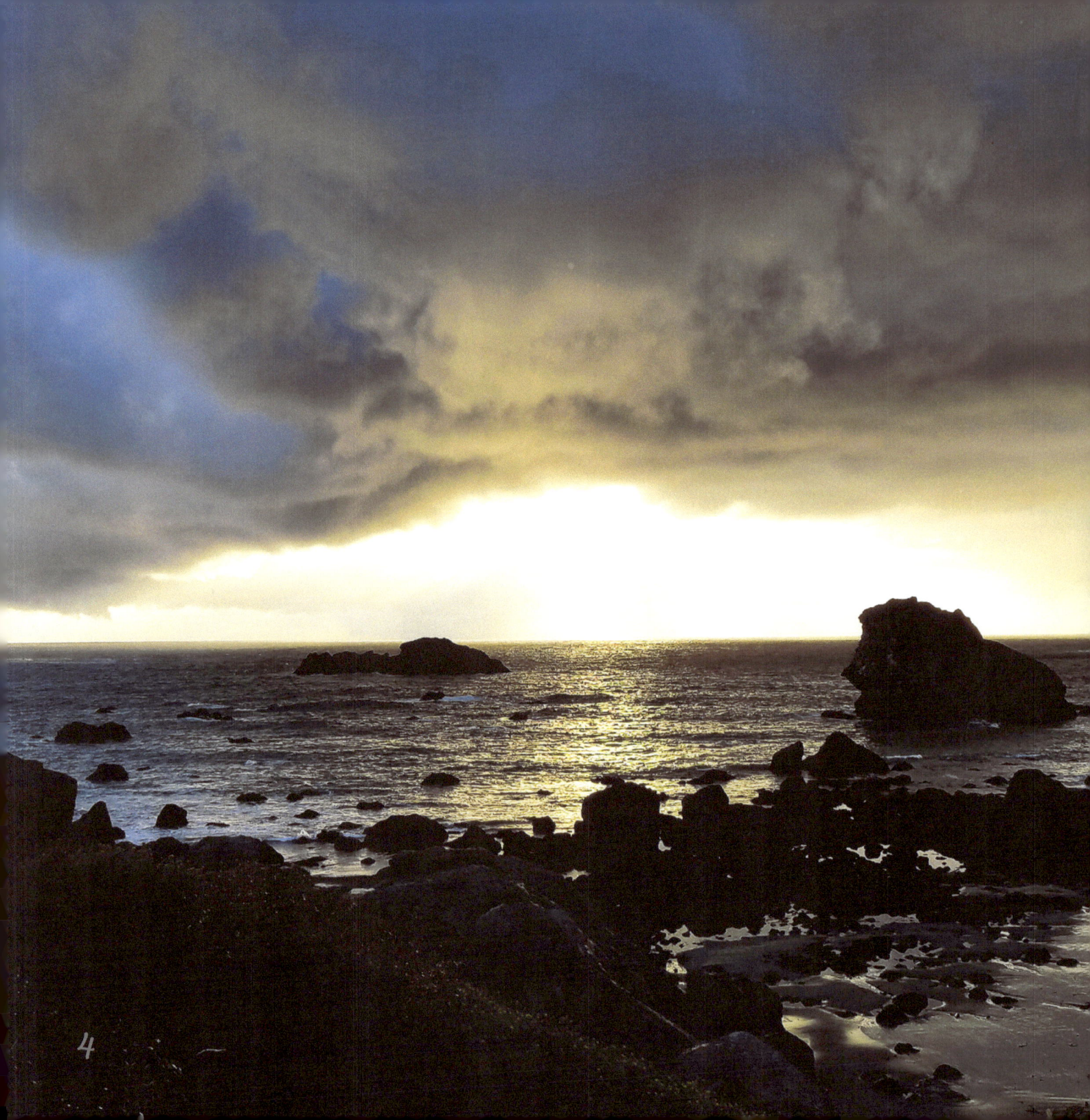

We discovered the Pacific Northwest Coast while visiting friends. Within three months, we sold our home and bought a home in Crescent City, California. This was the fall of 2016. The opportunity to live by the ocean was my dream come true.

I marveled at the variety of sunsets and sunrises that occurred most days, and dug out old cameras with a variety of lenses to capture the stunning show.

Most of these photos are taken at Pebble Beach and South Beach in Crescent City. A few photos were taken just south of Crescent City in the Klamath area.

I am excited to share the beauty of this pristine area and document God's gift to the world. Each one a frozen moment in time.

Karen Arnpriester

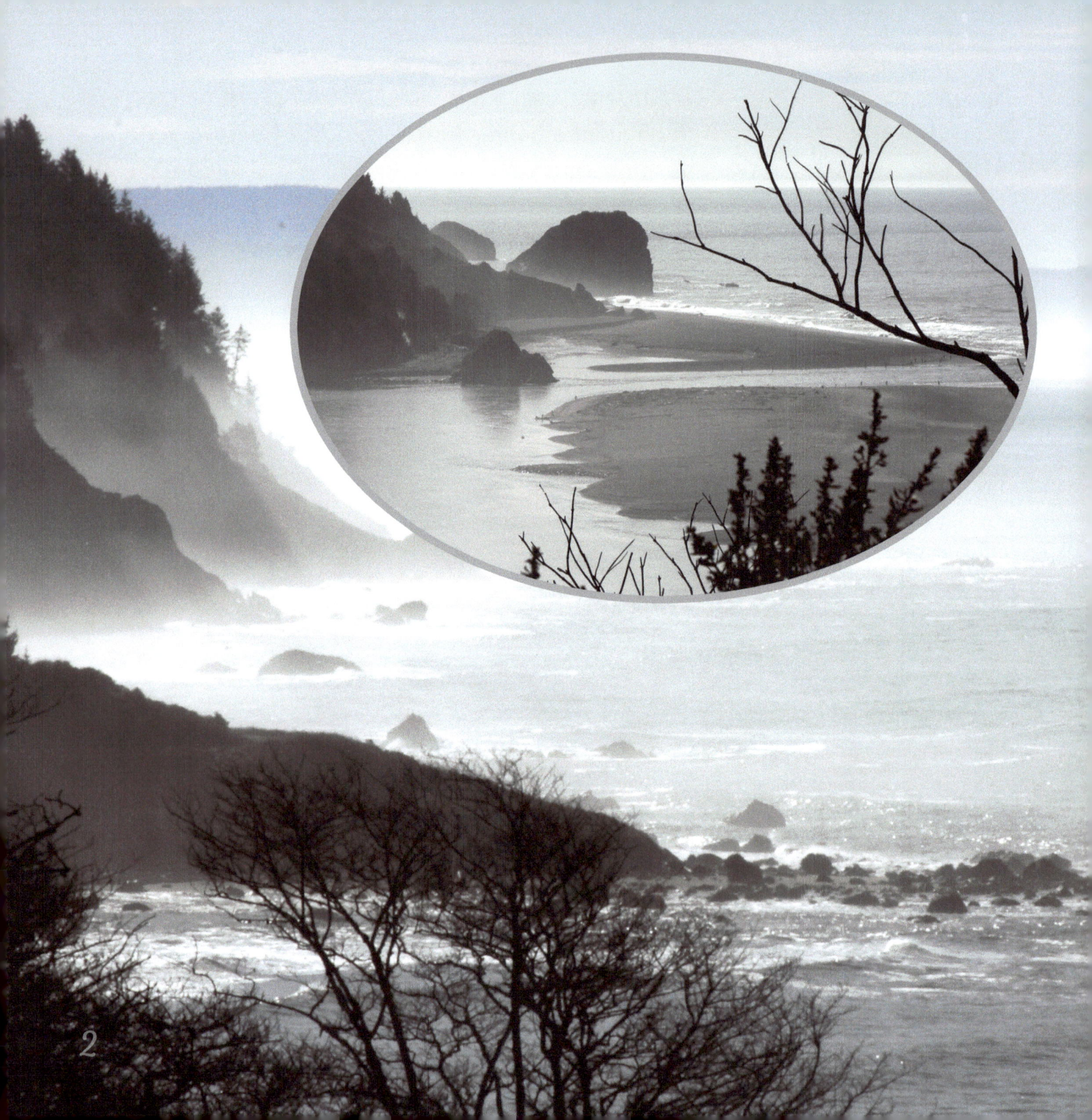

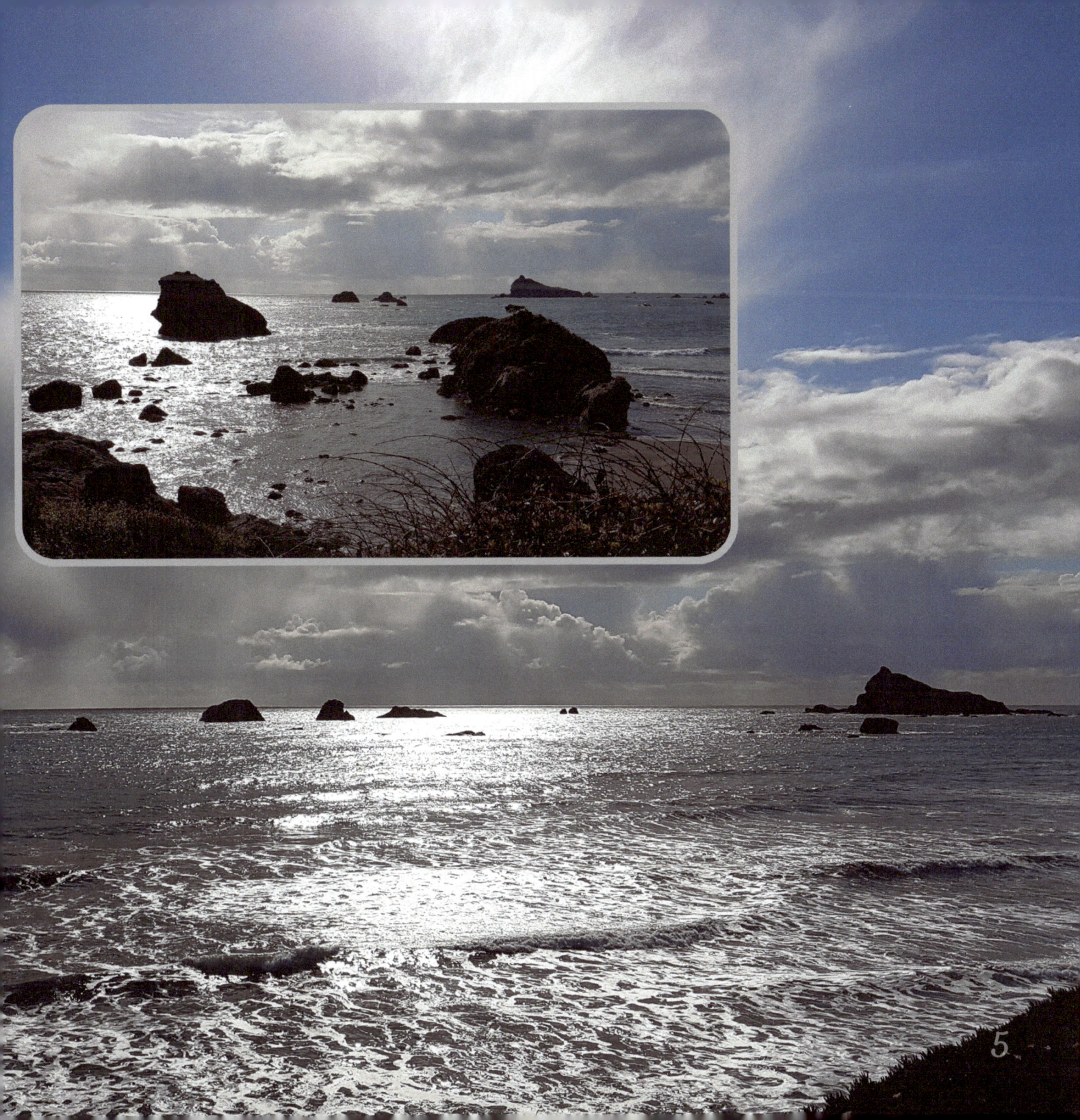

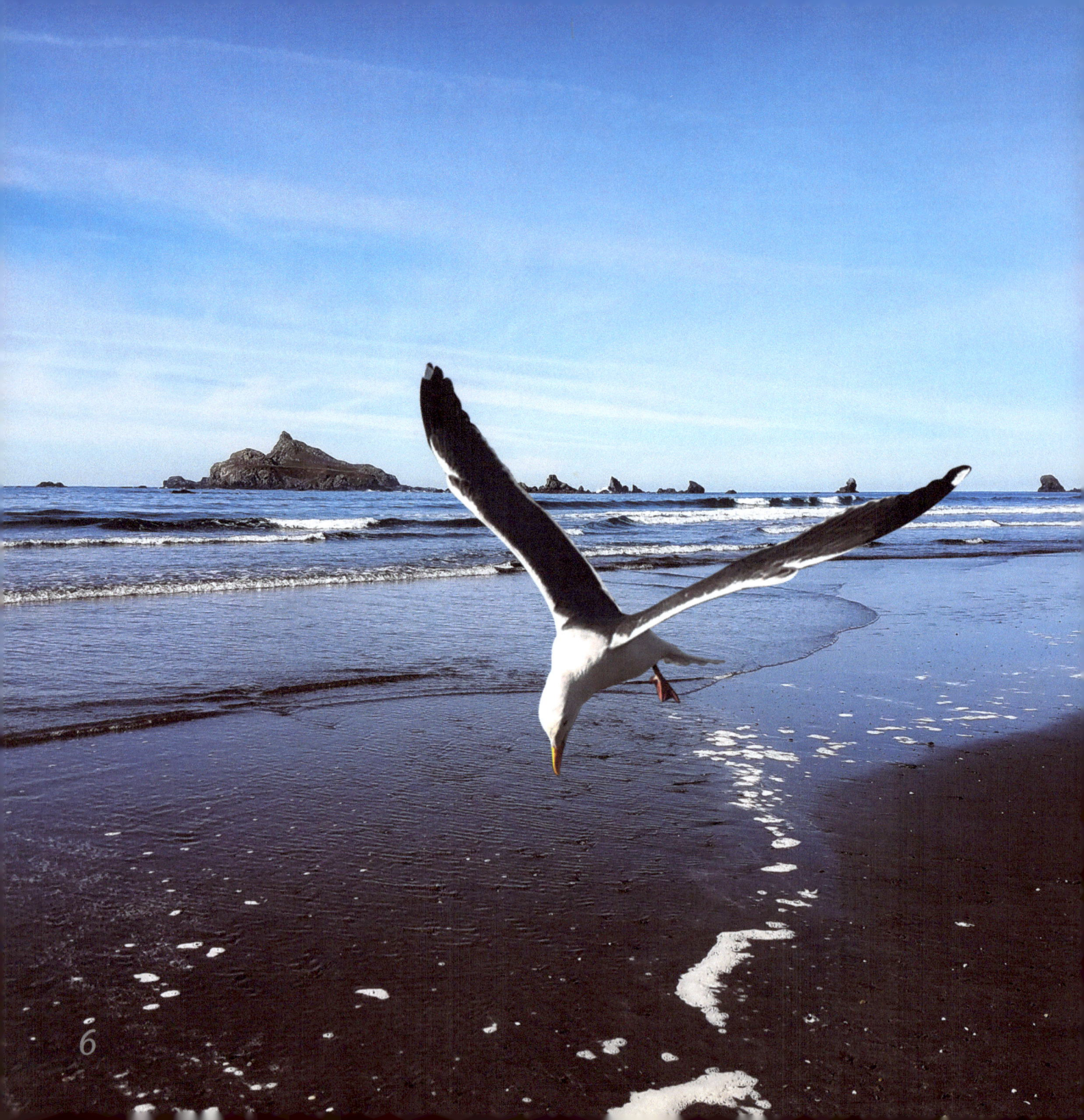

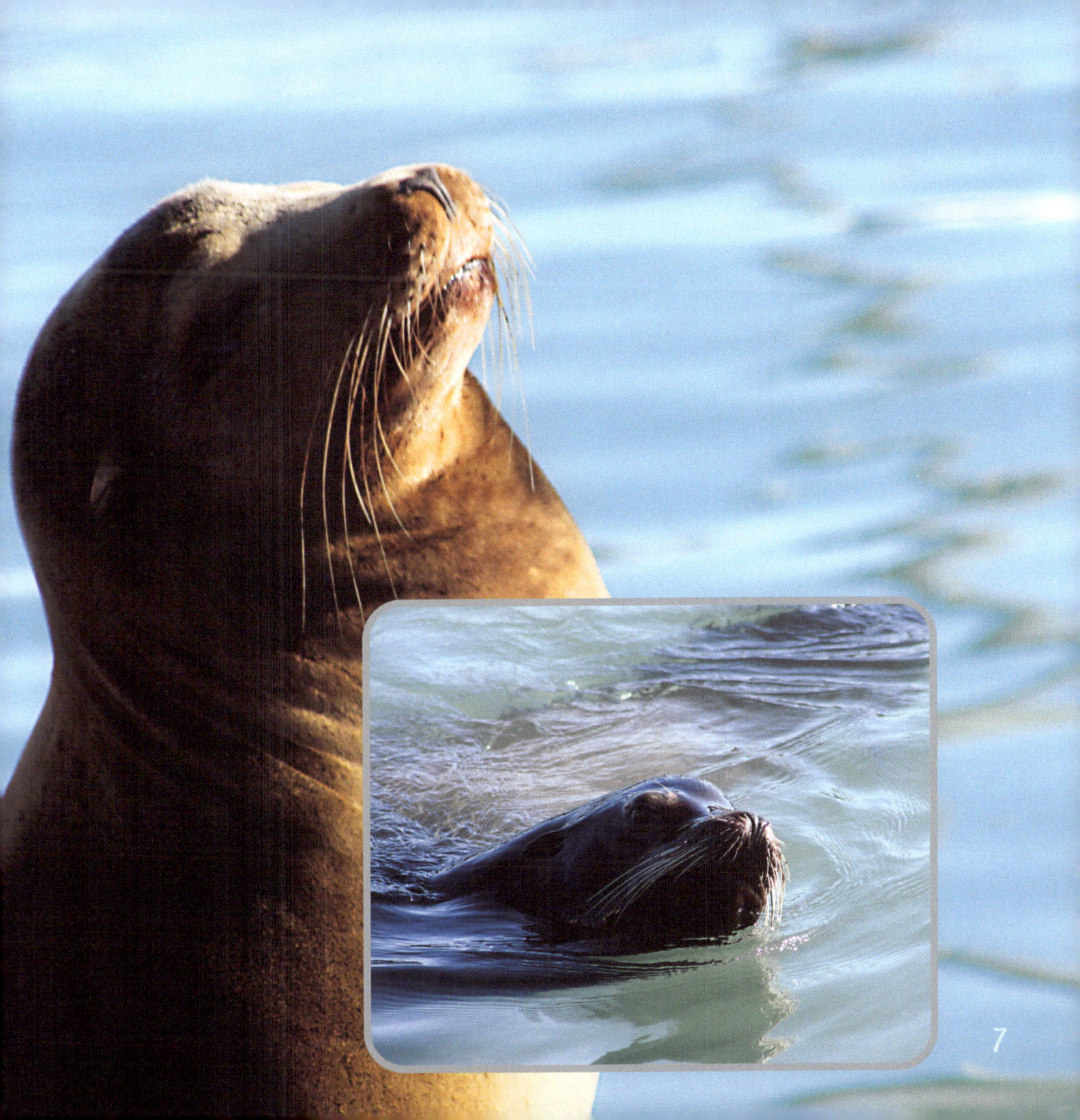

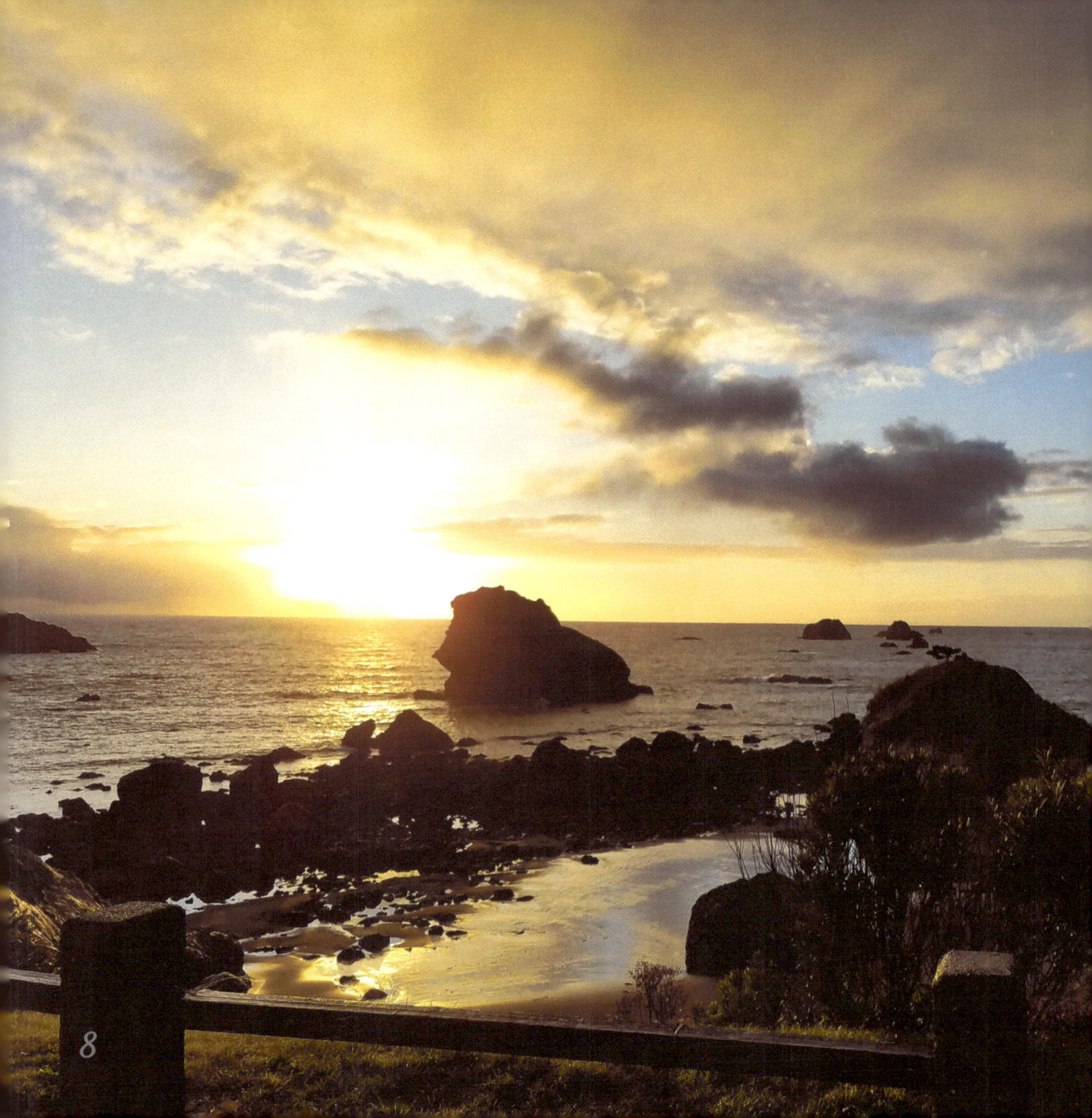

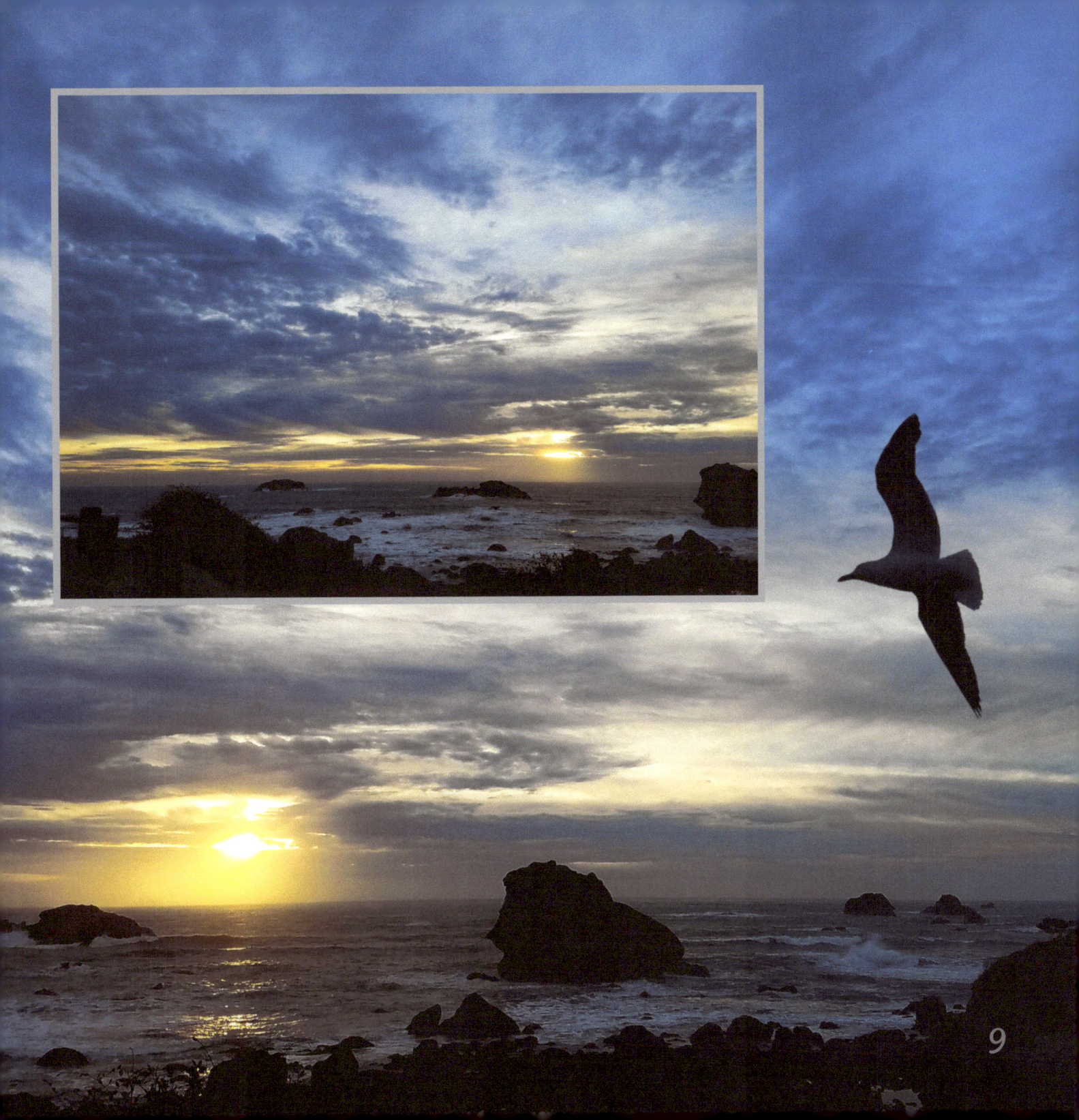

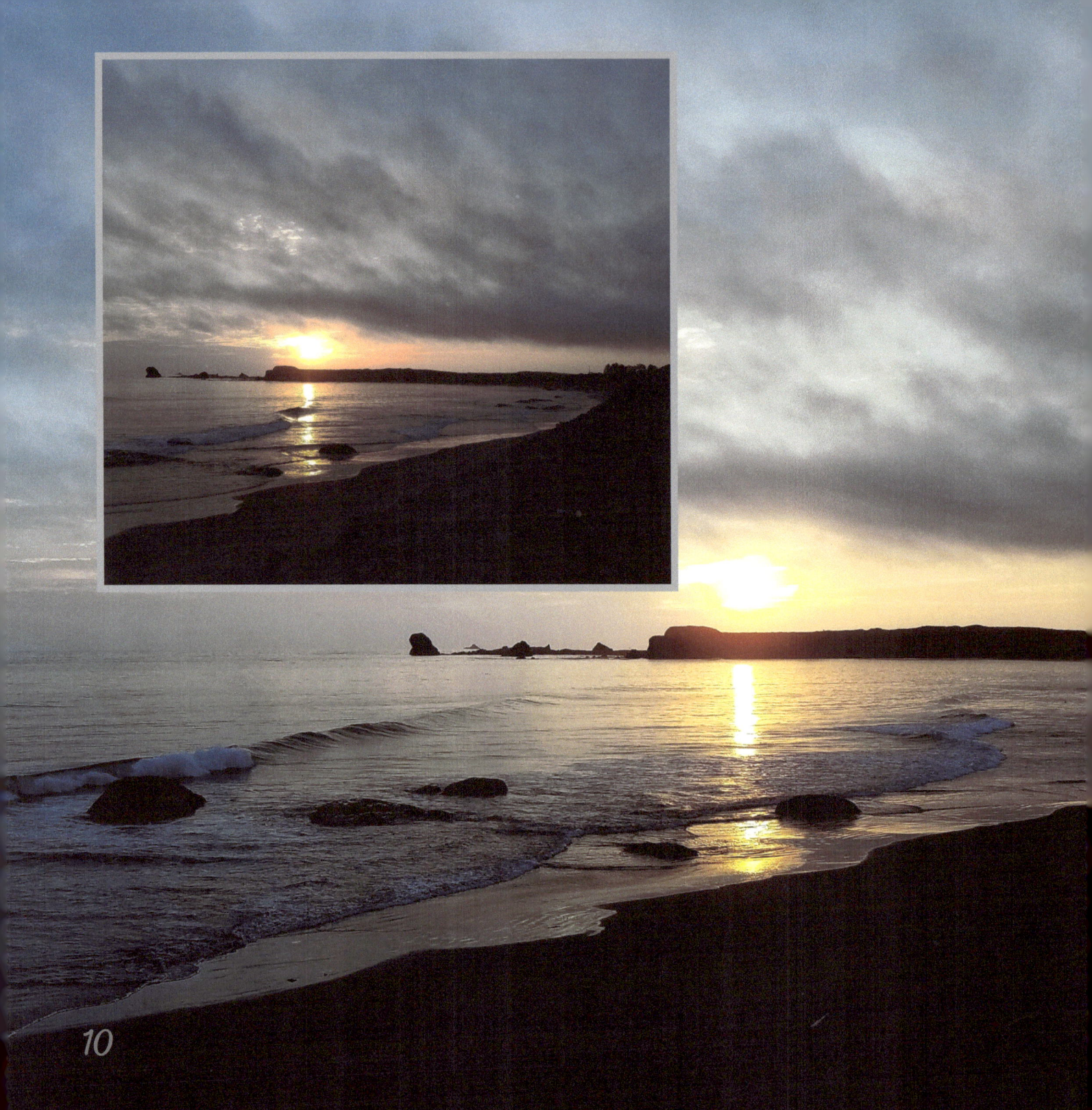

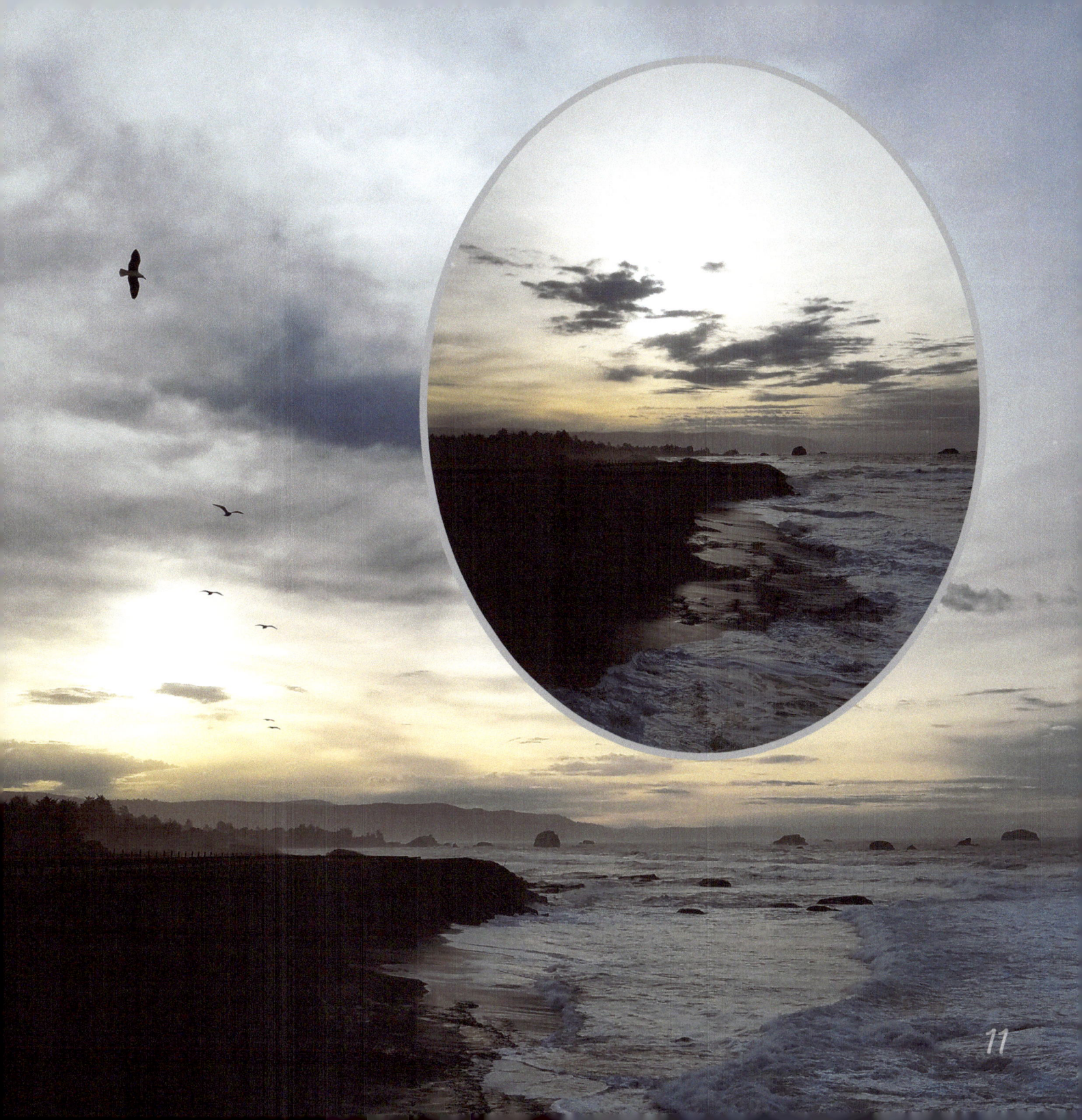

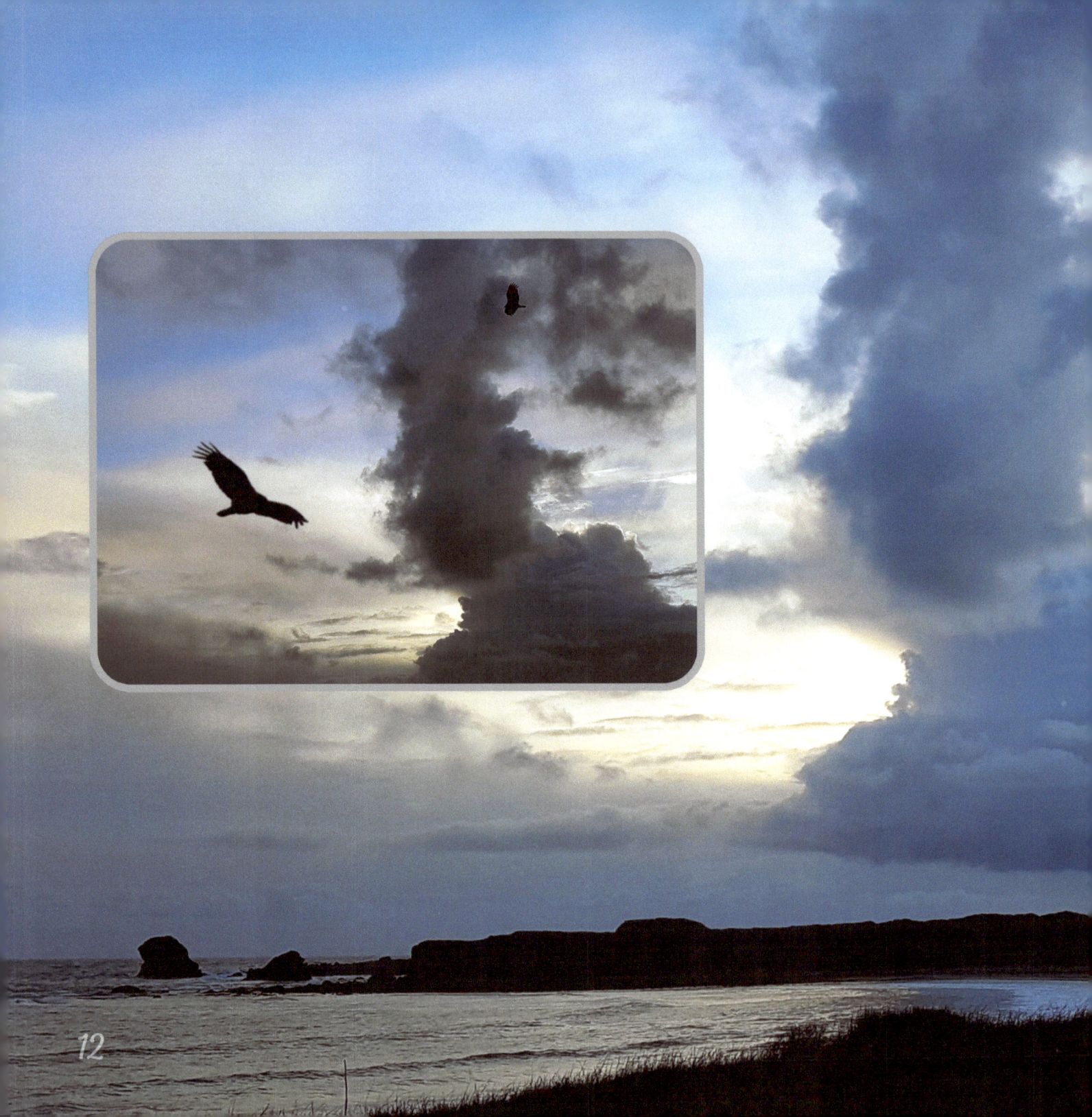

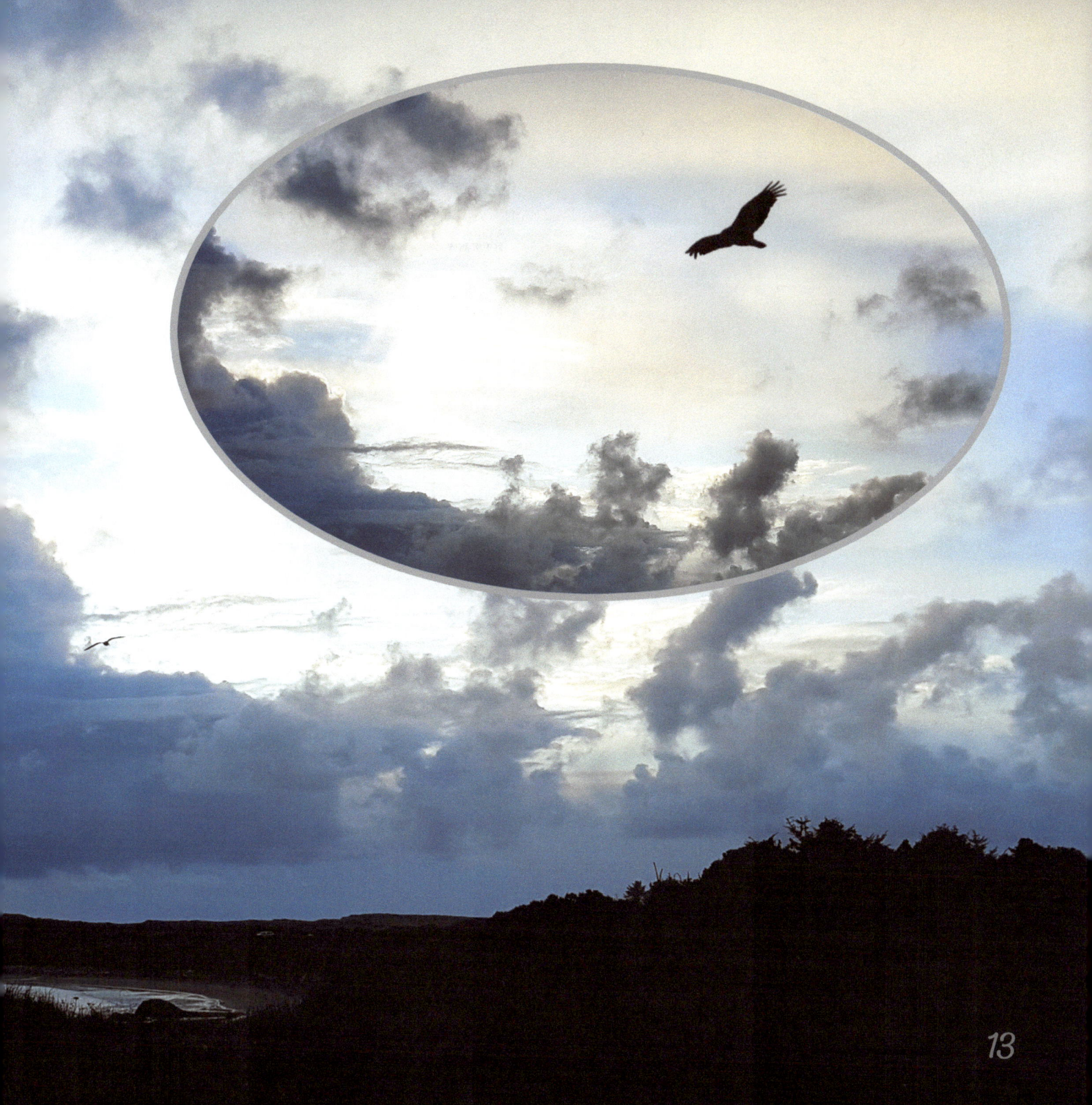

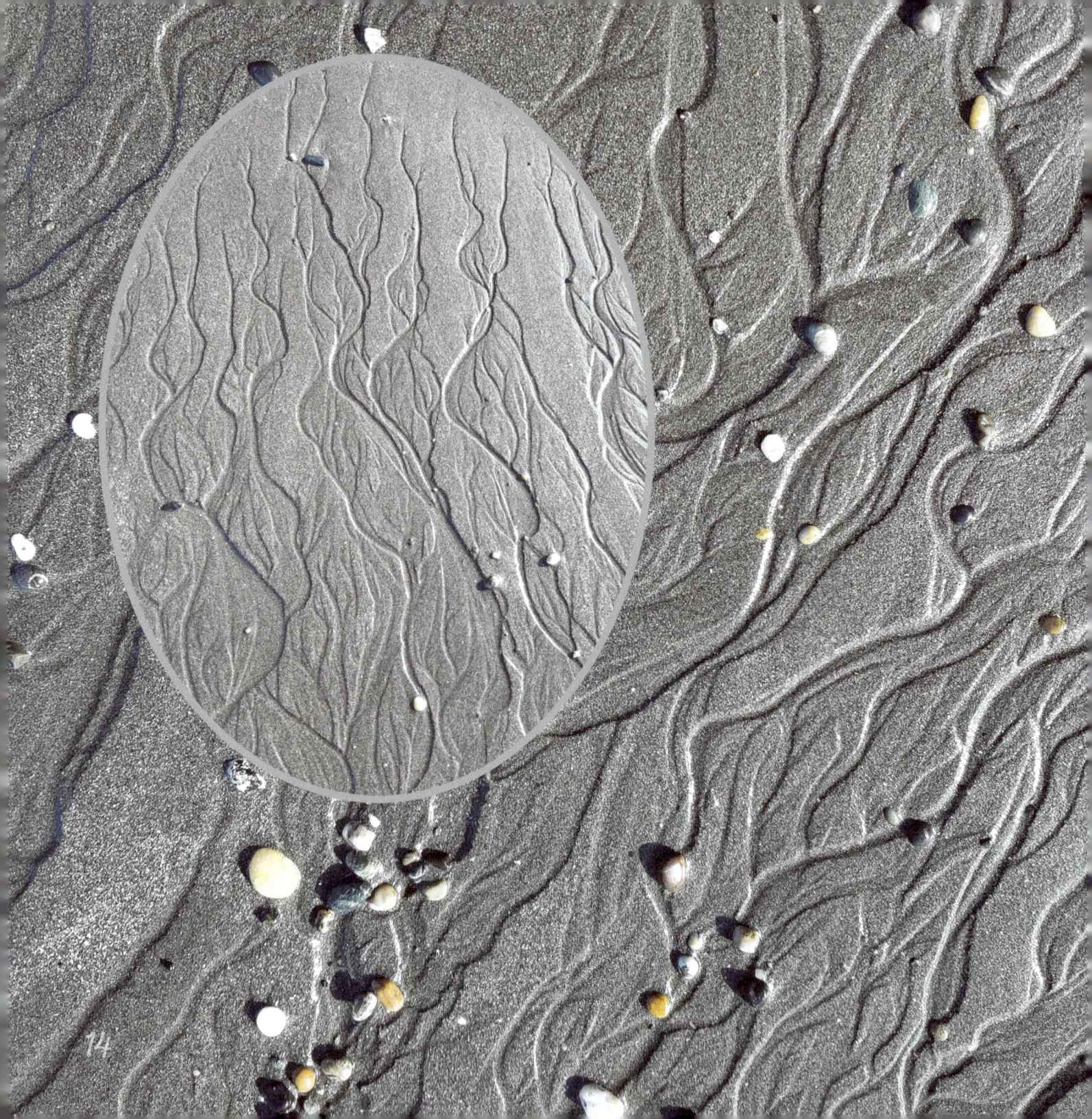

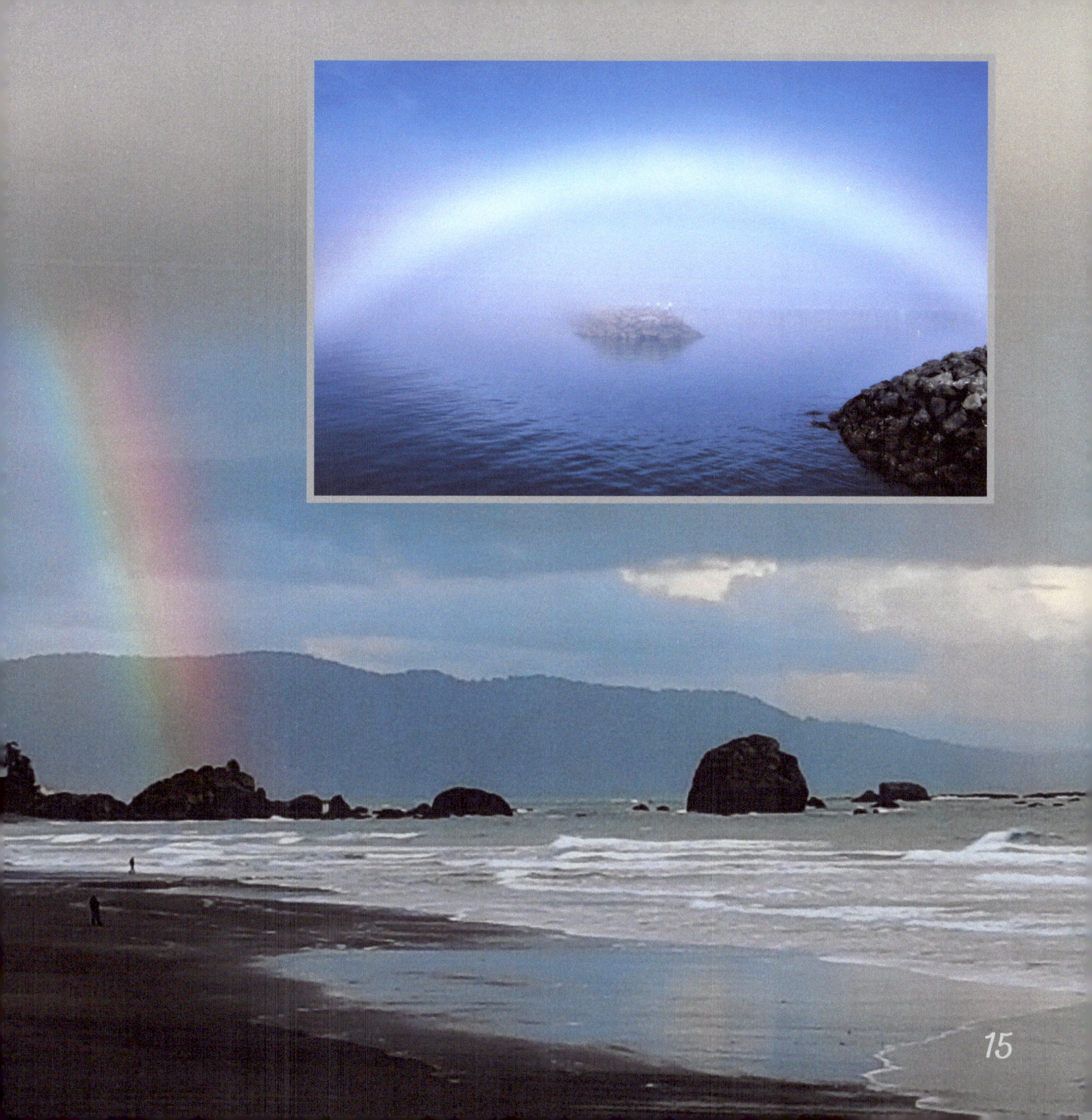

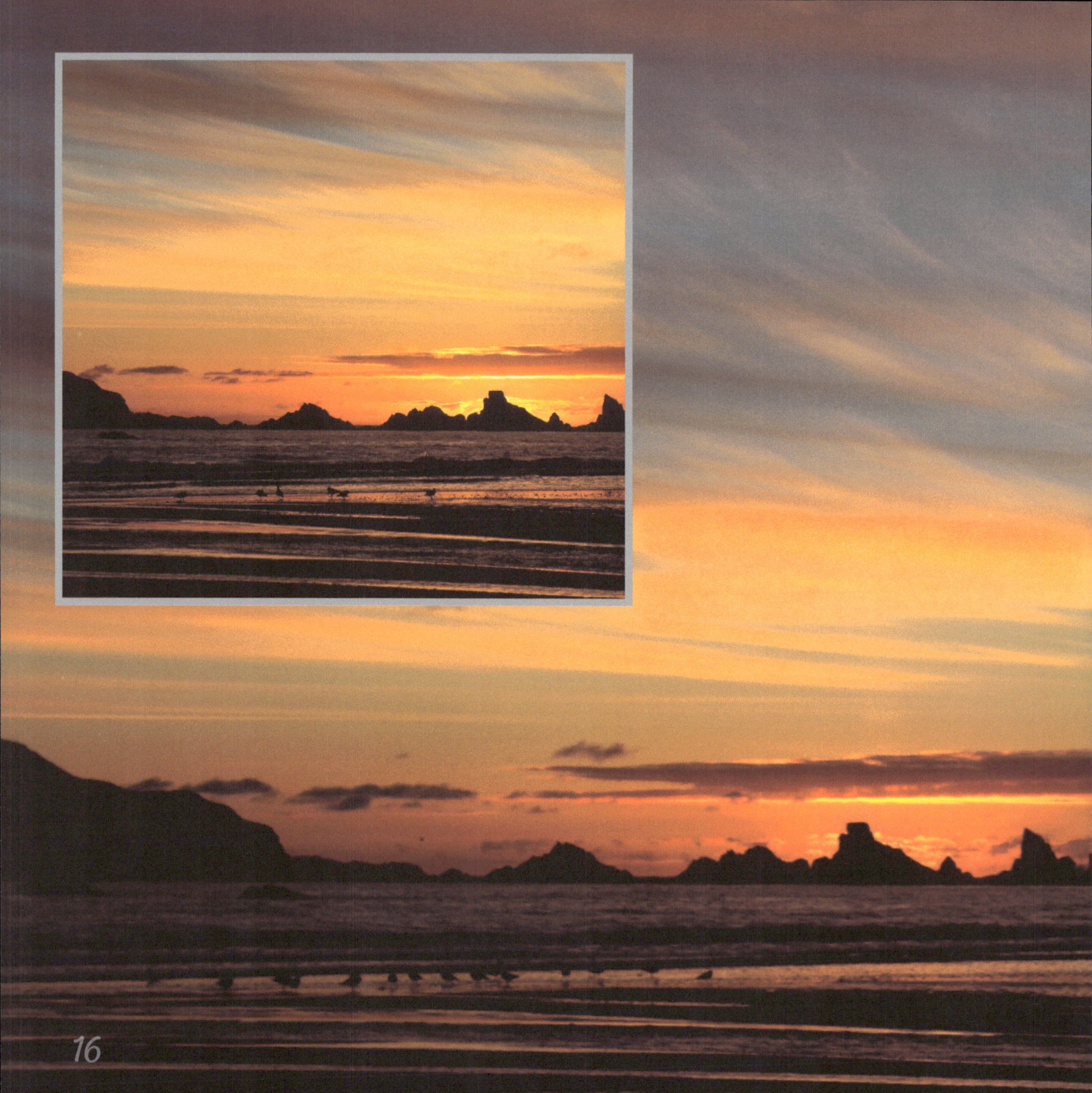

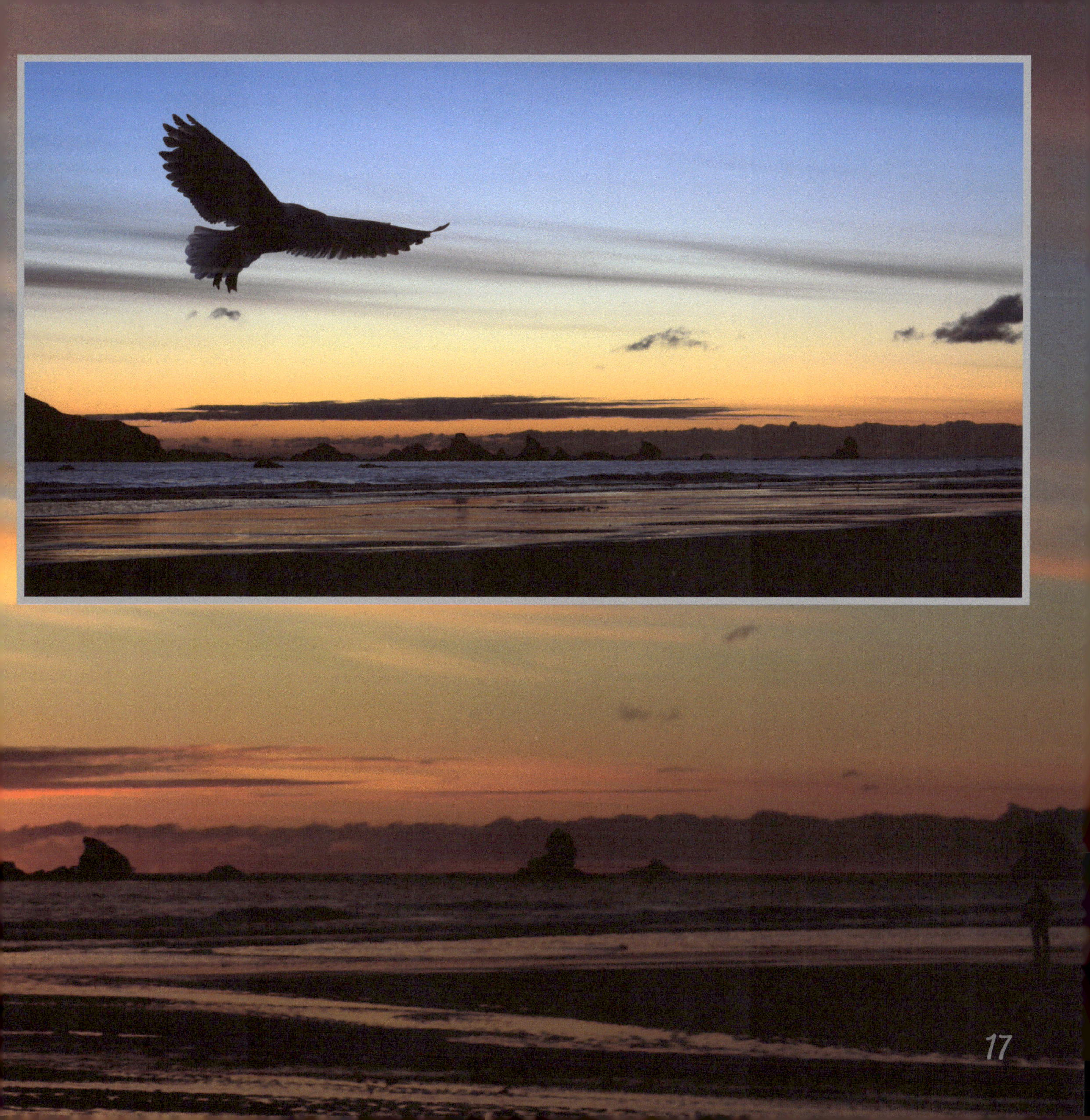

17

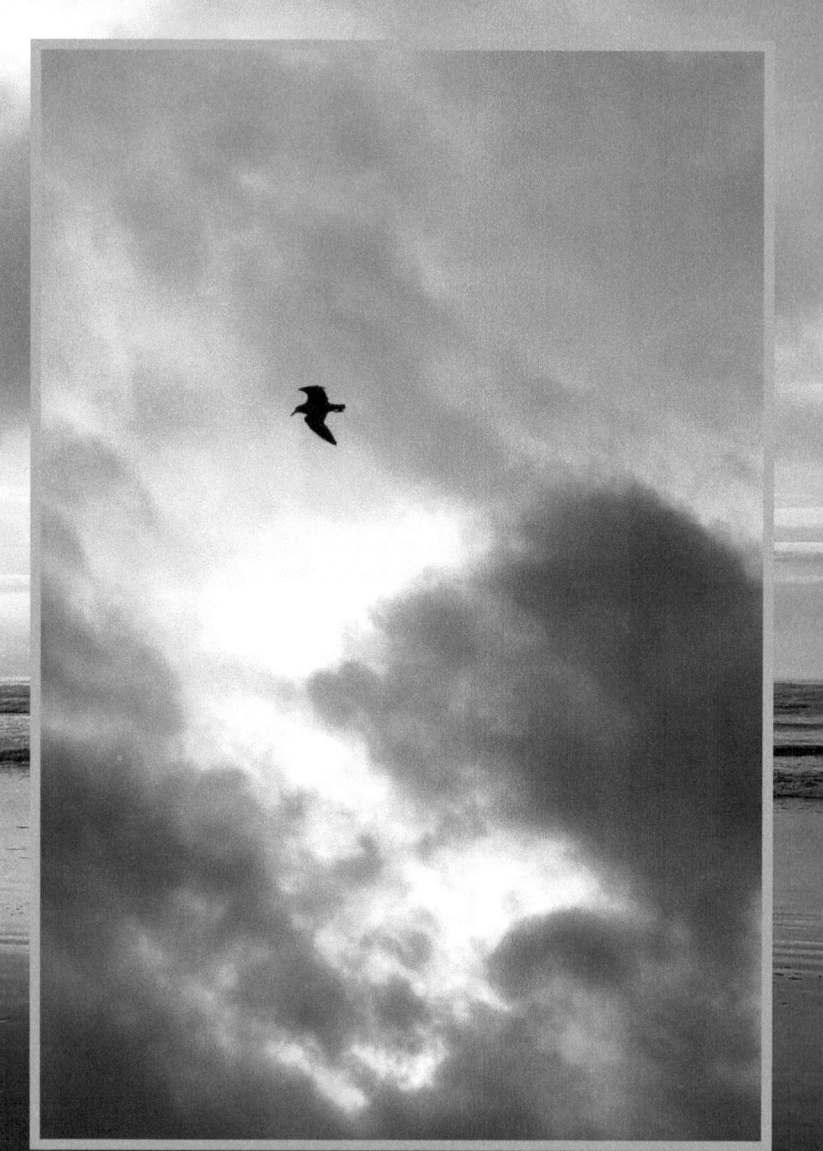

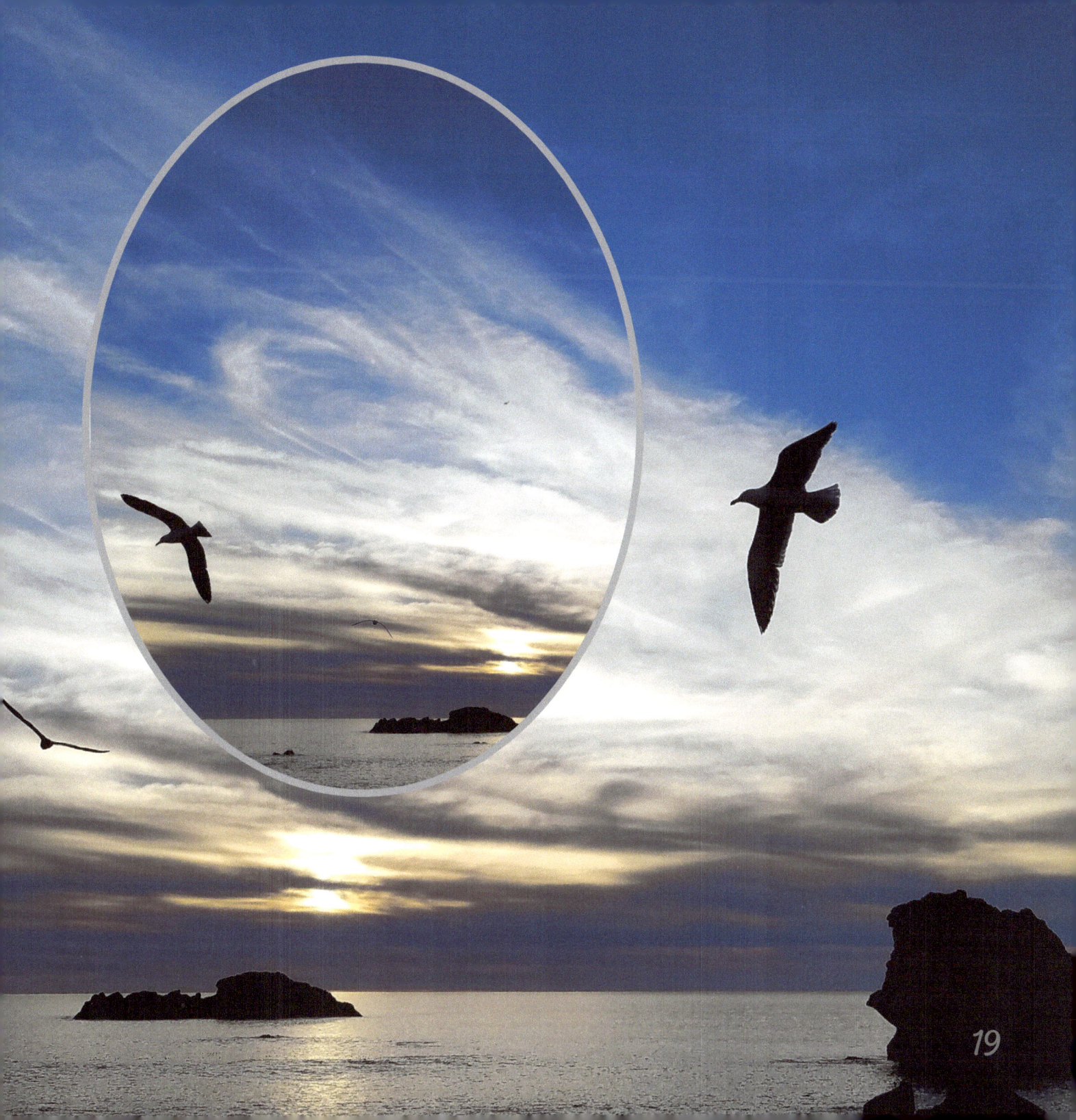

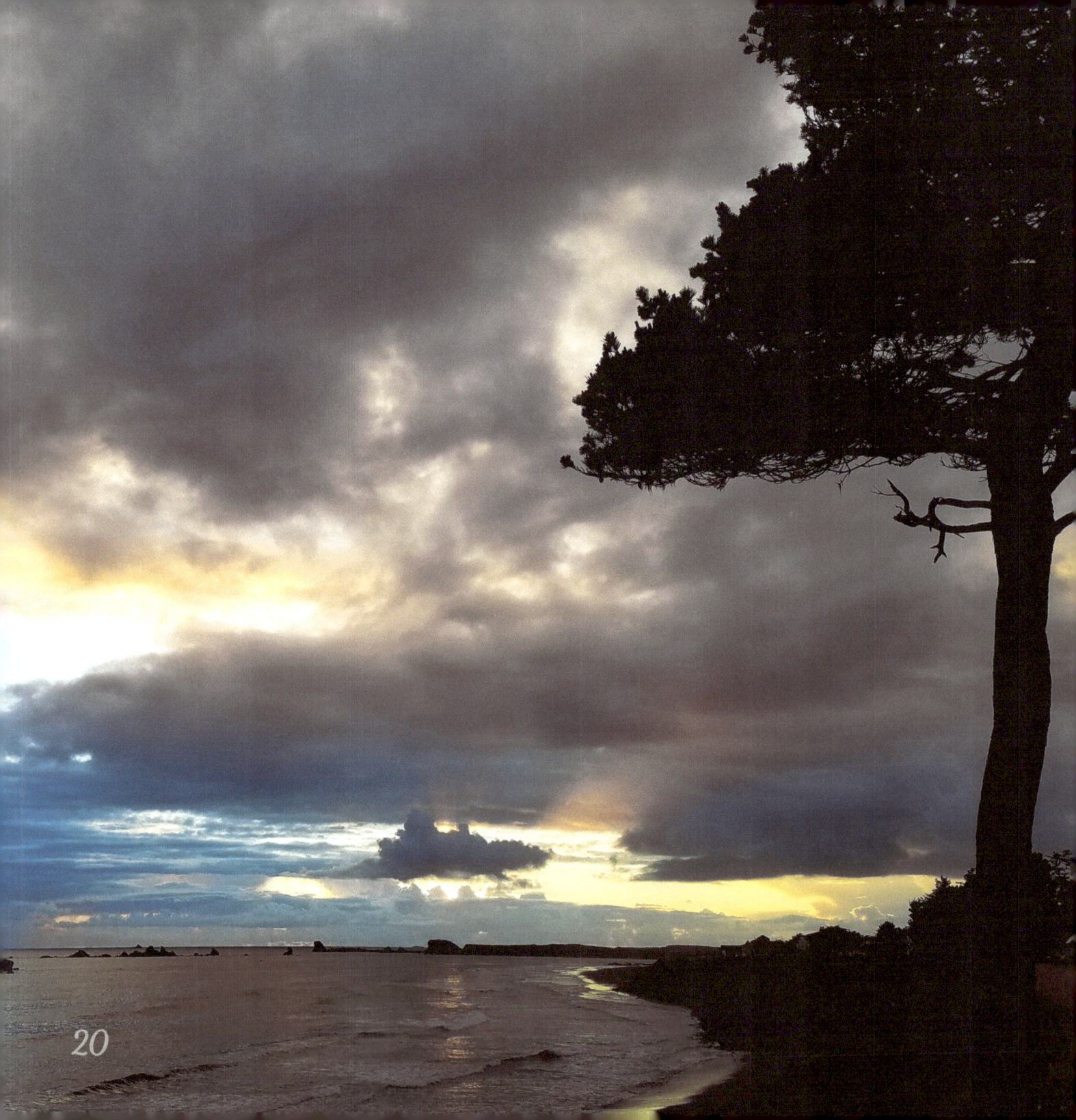

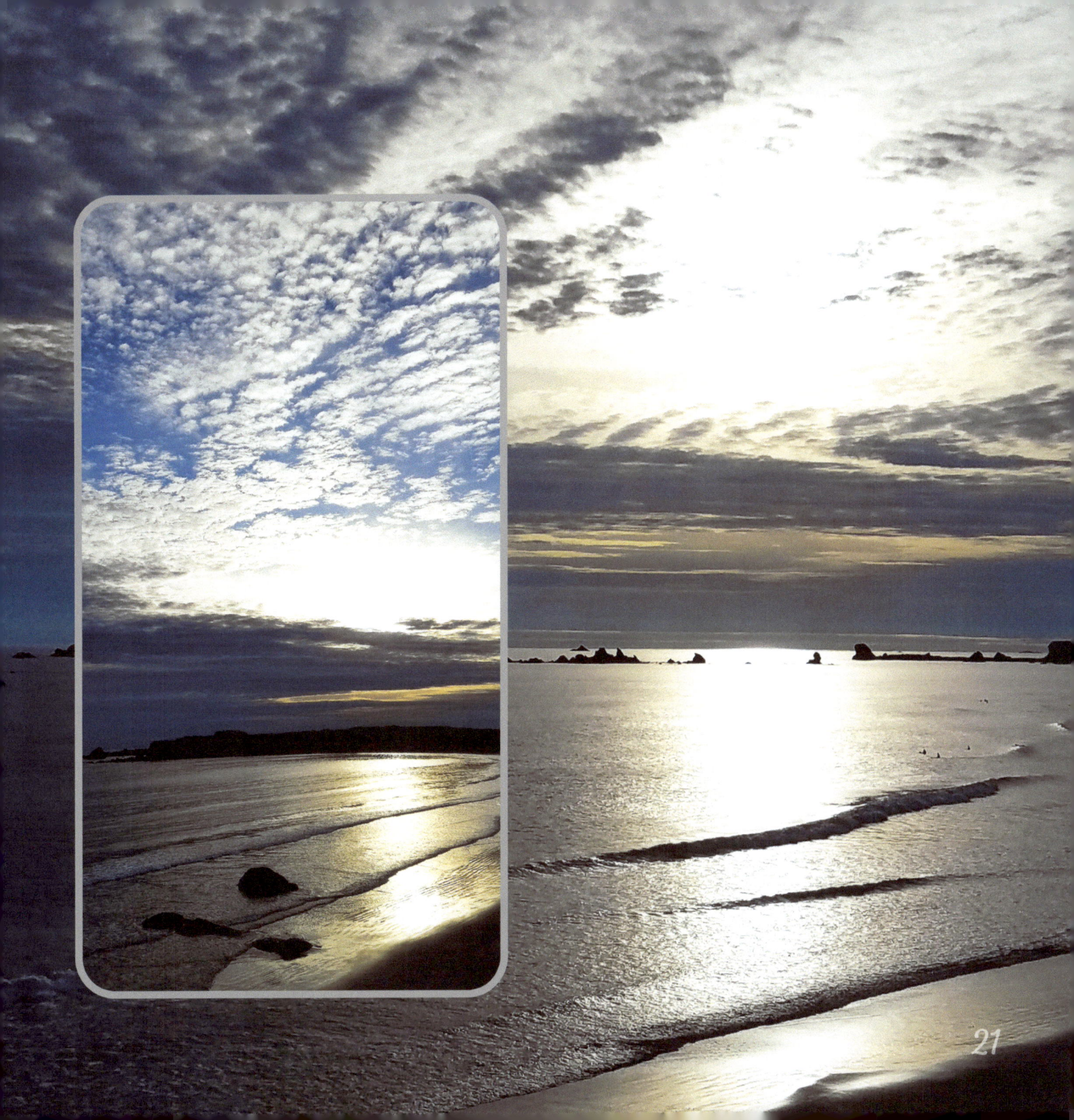

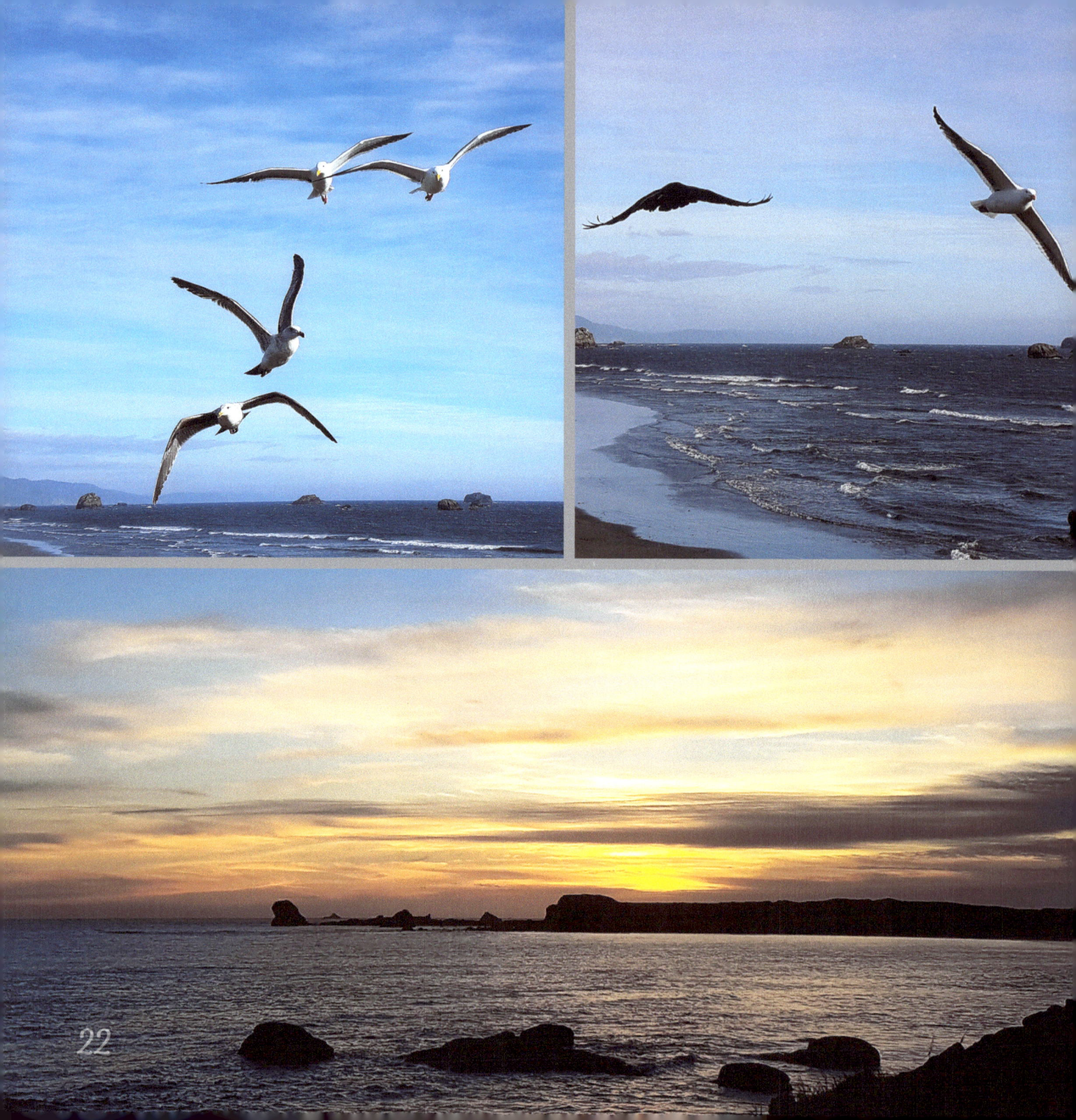

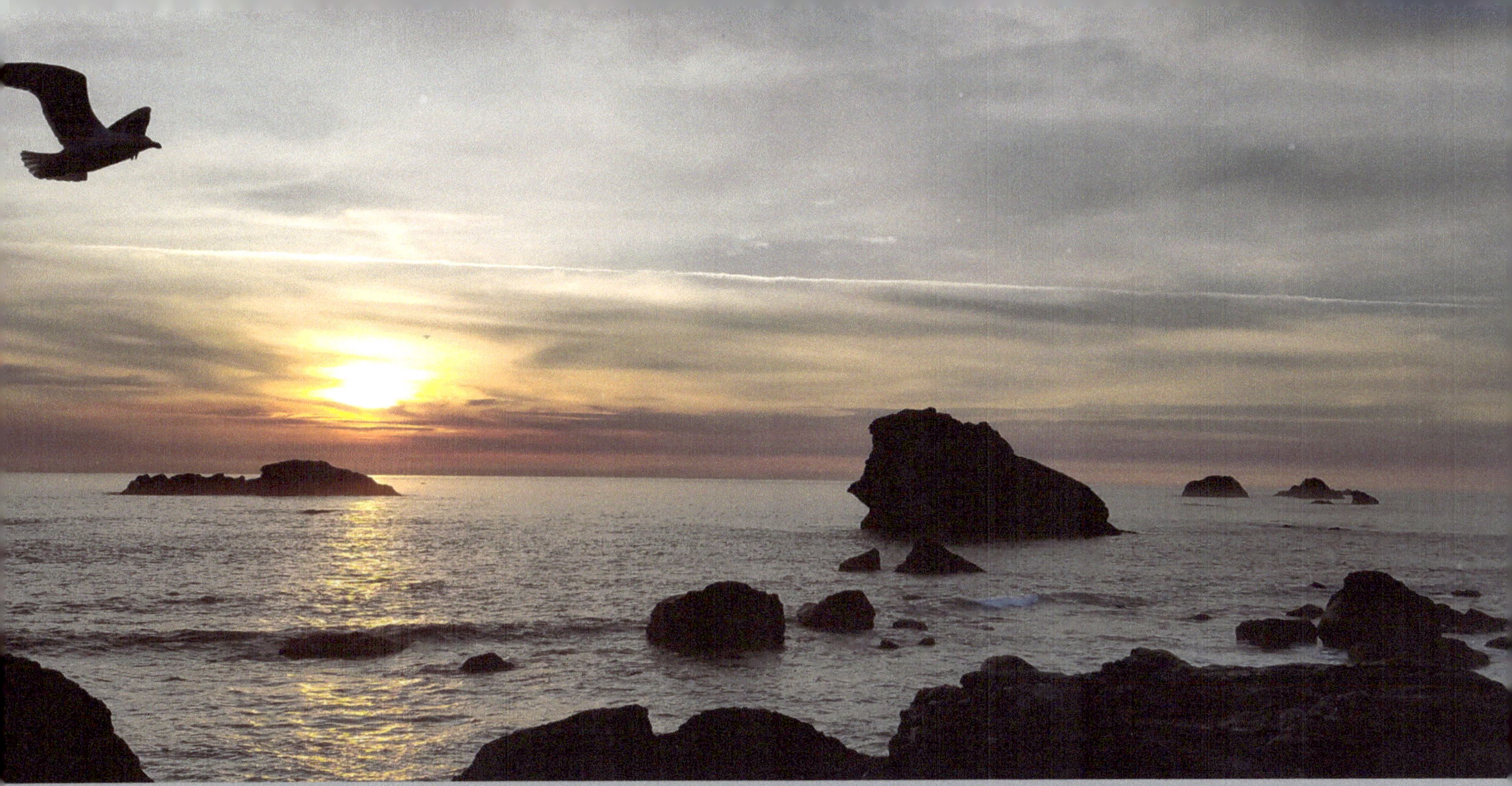

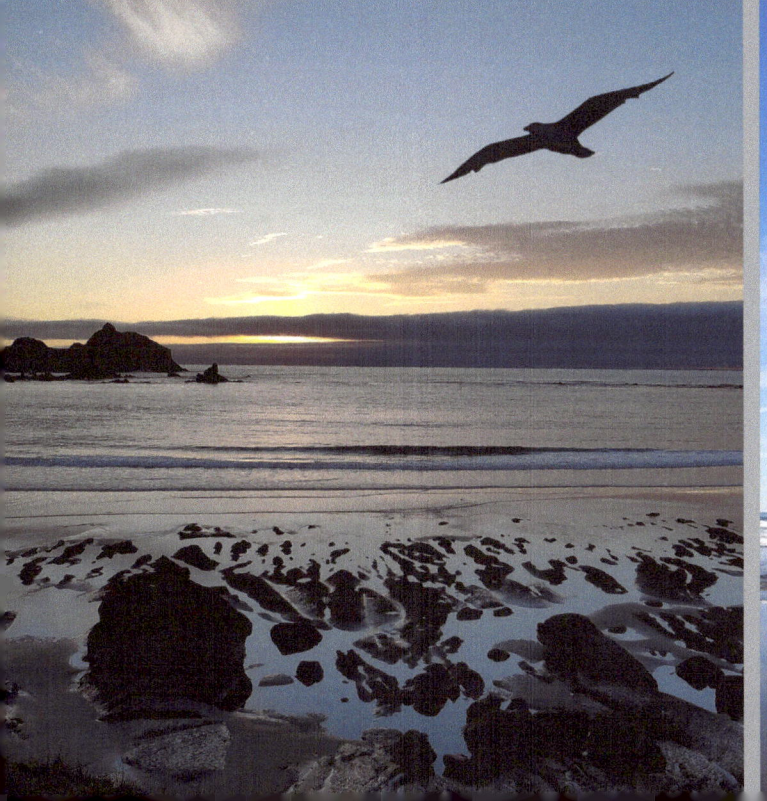
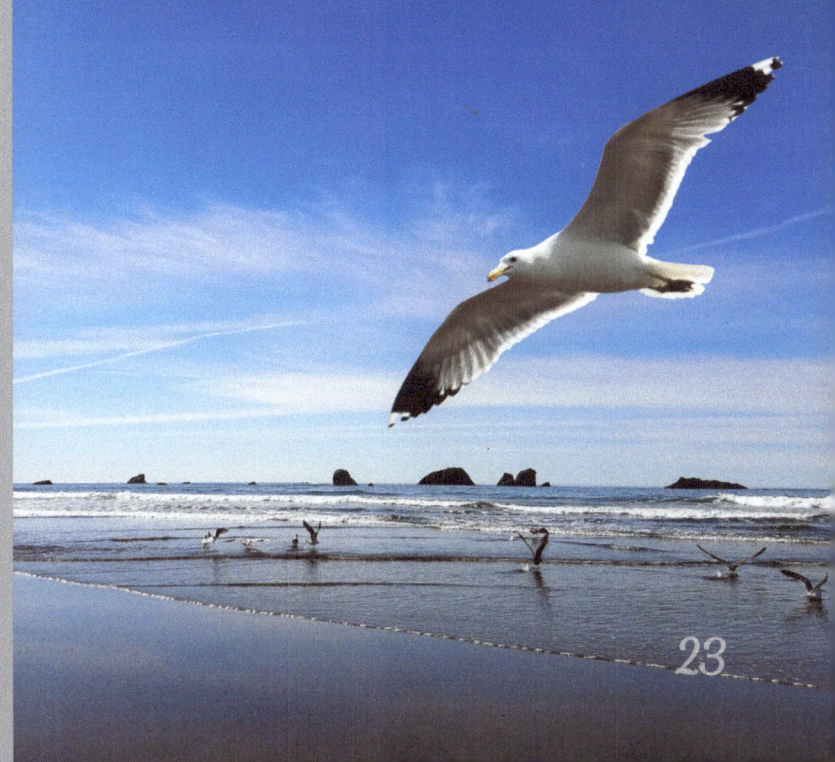

23

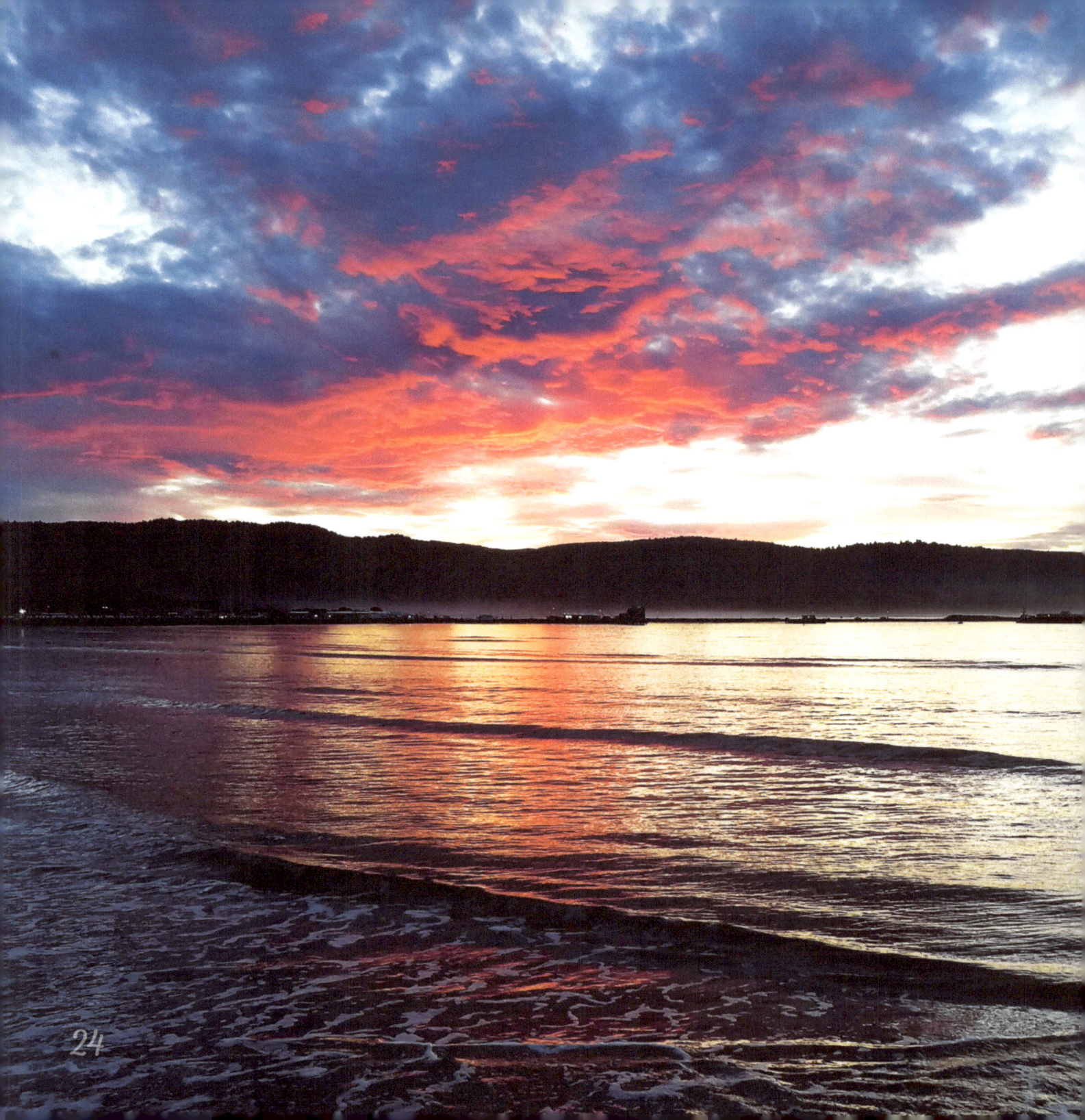

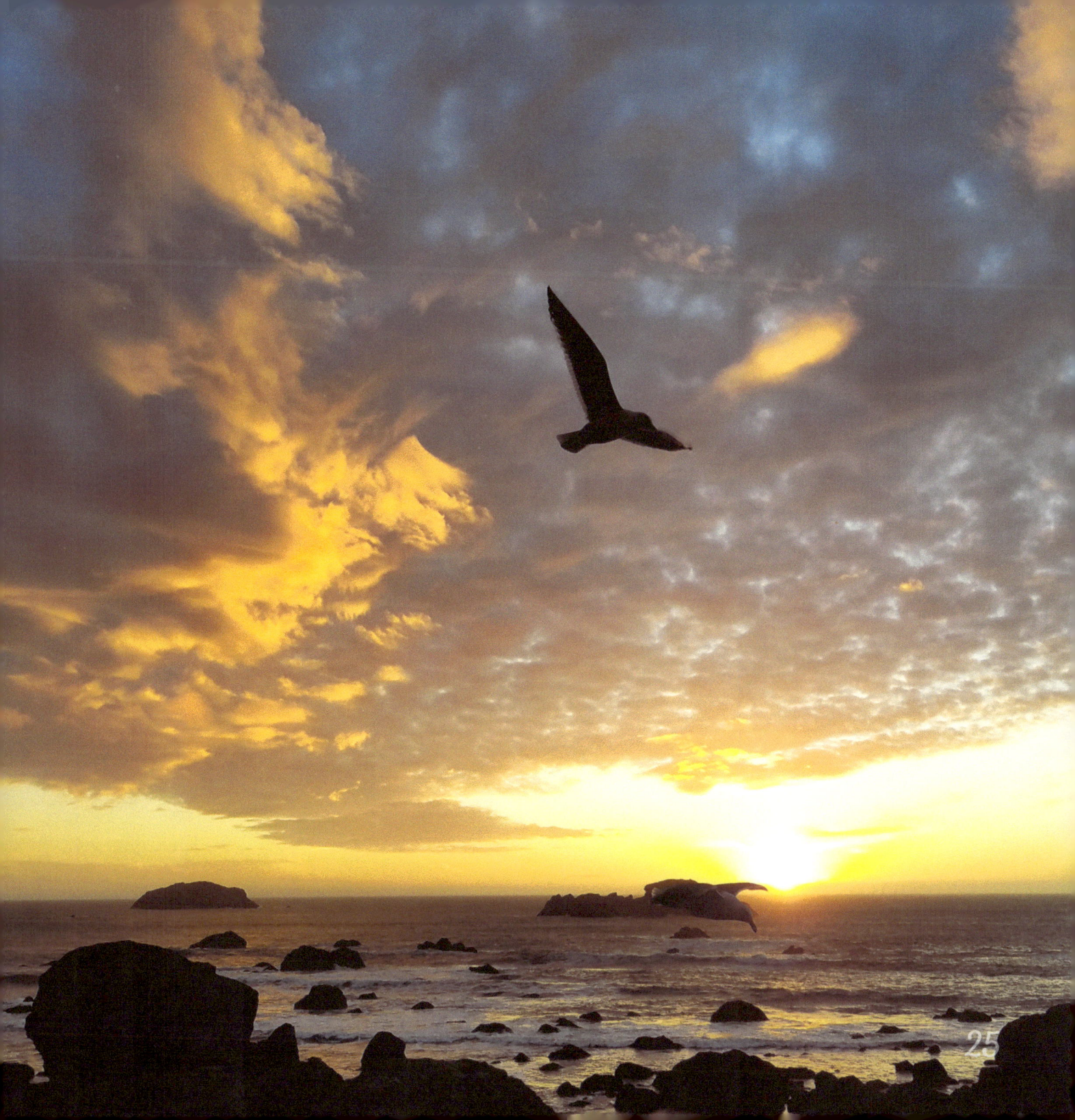

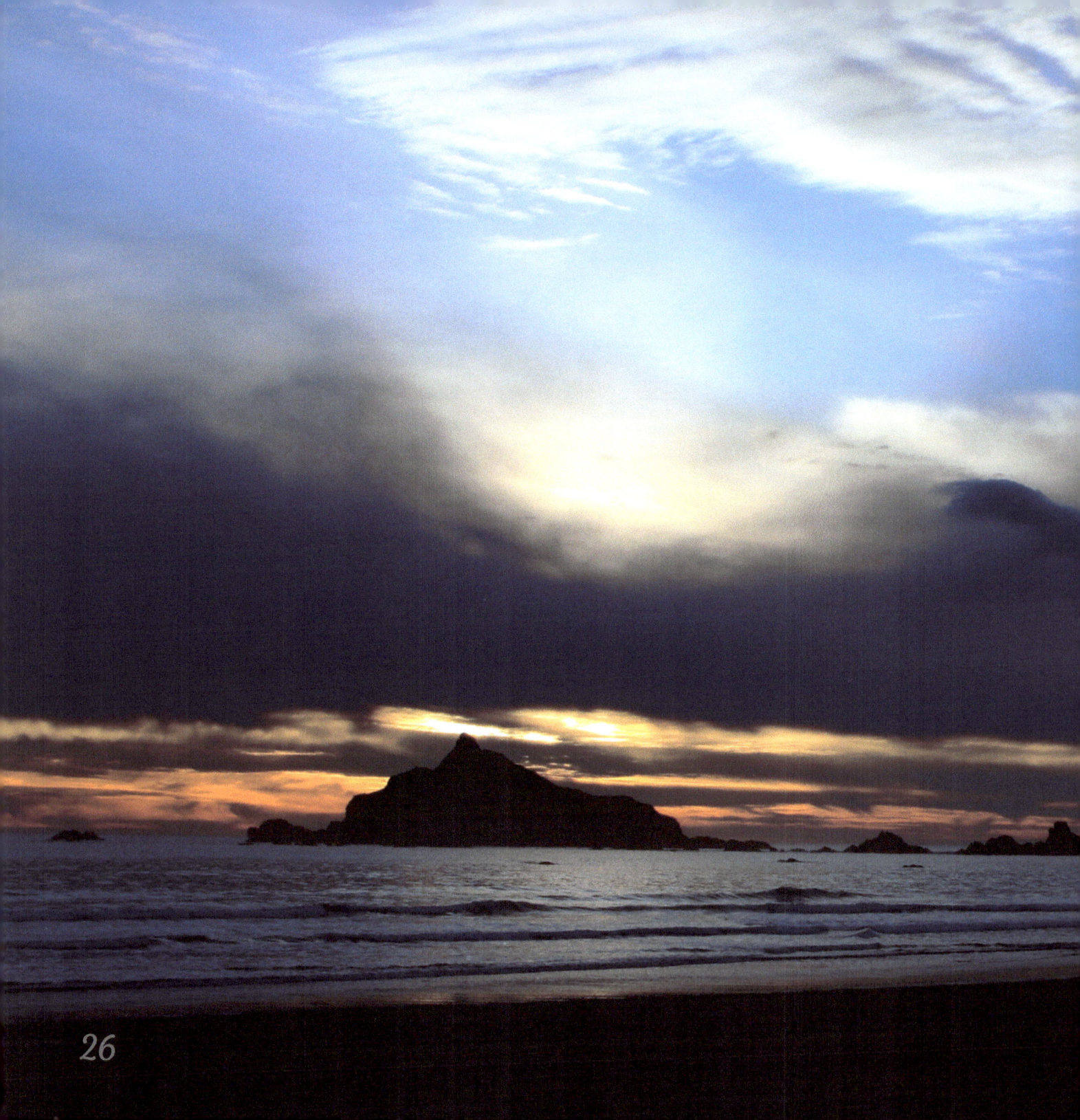

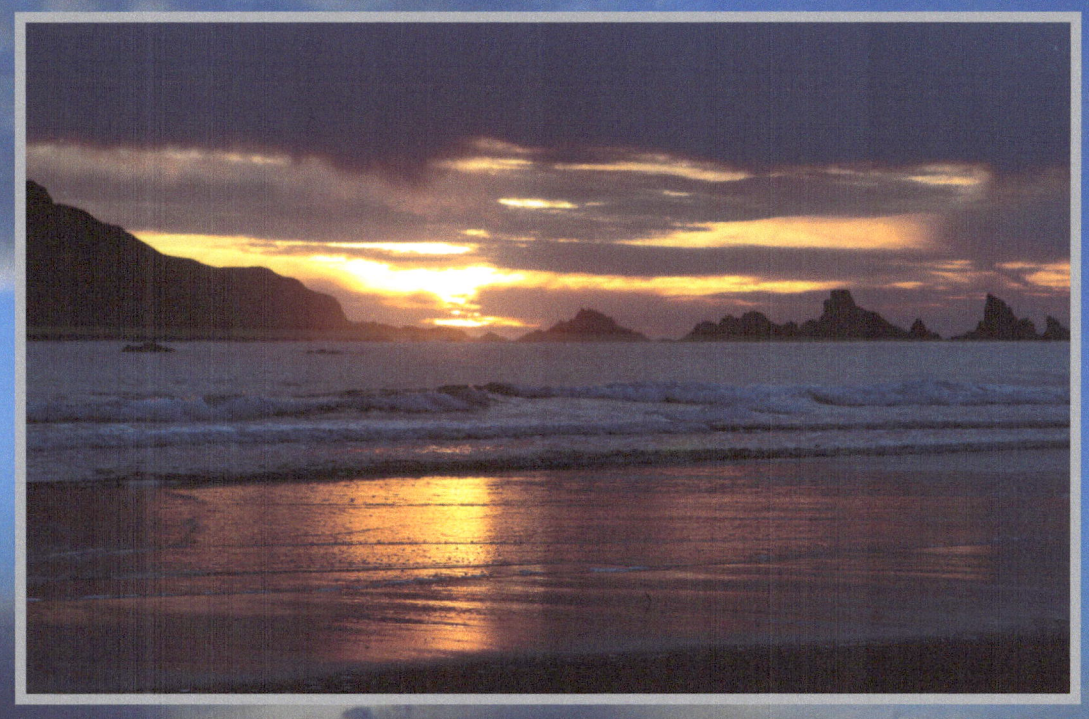
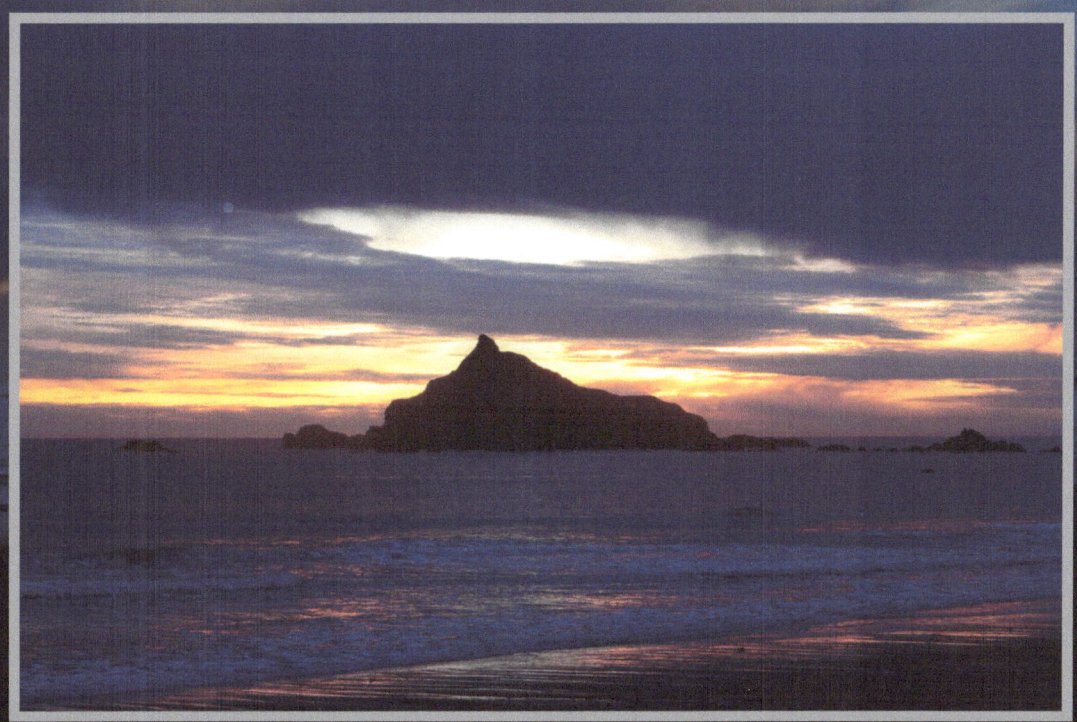

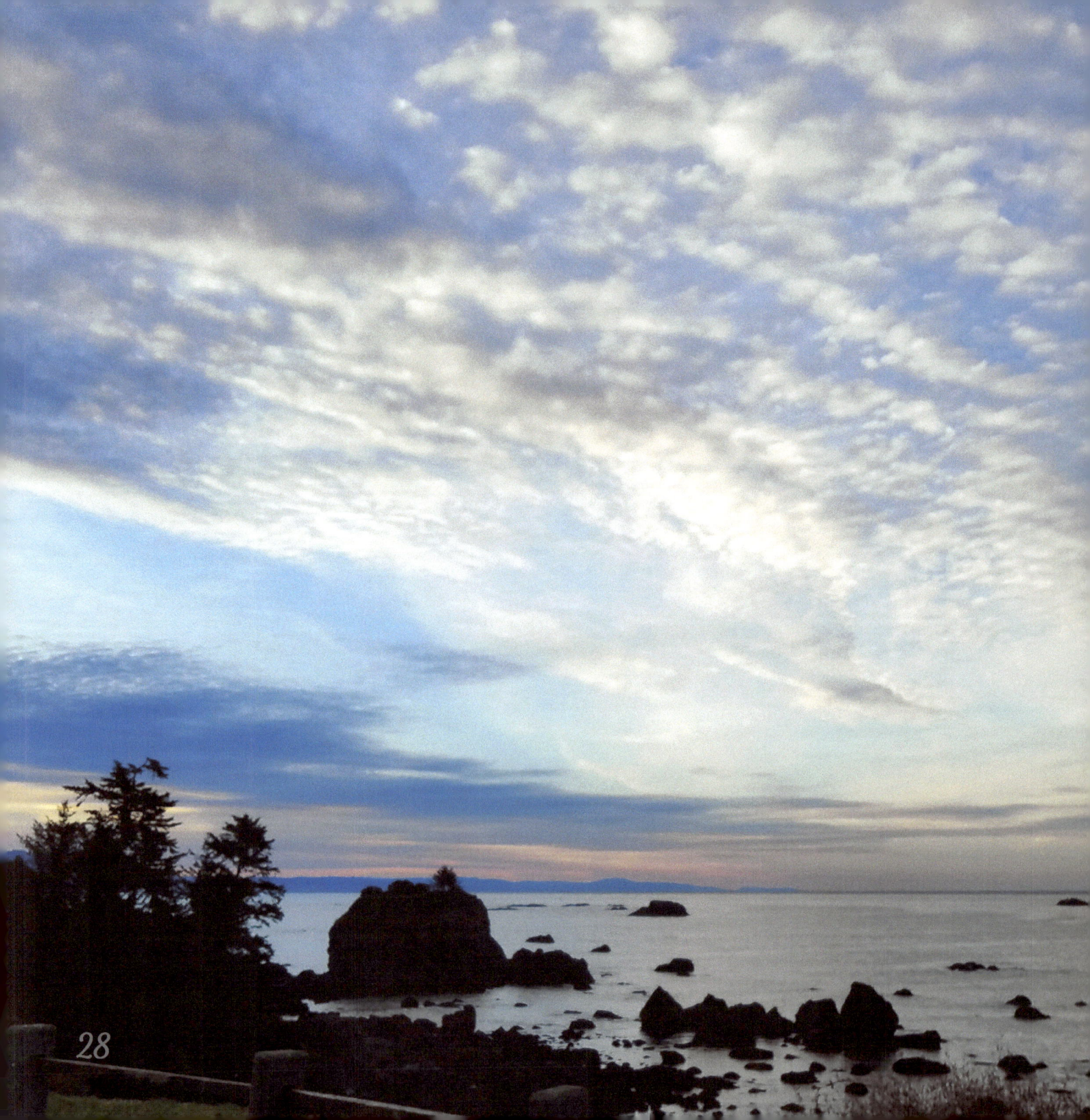

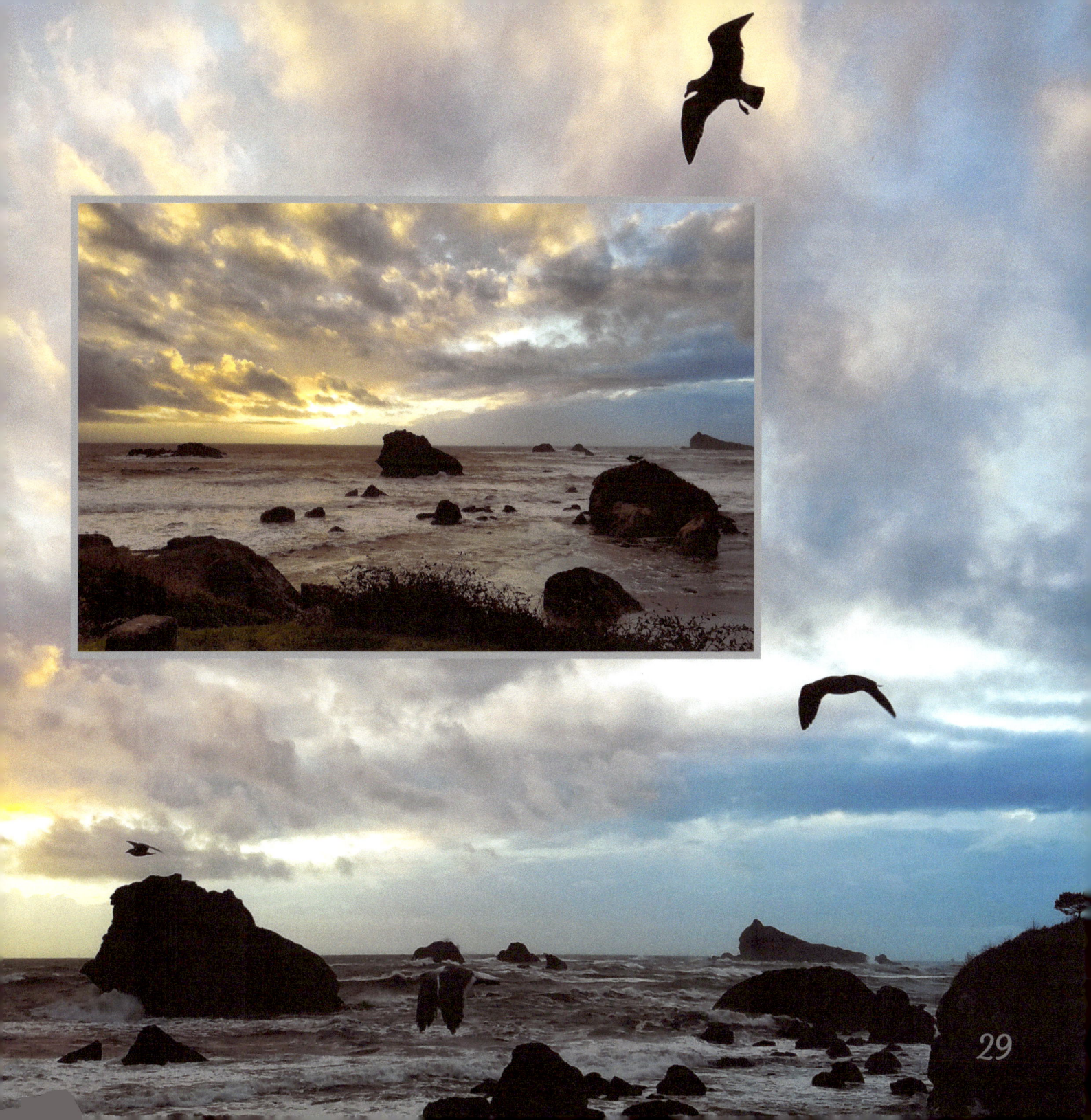

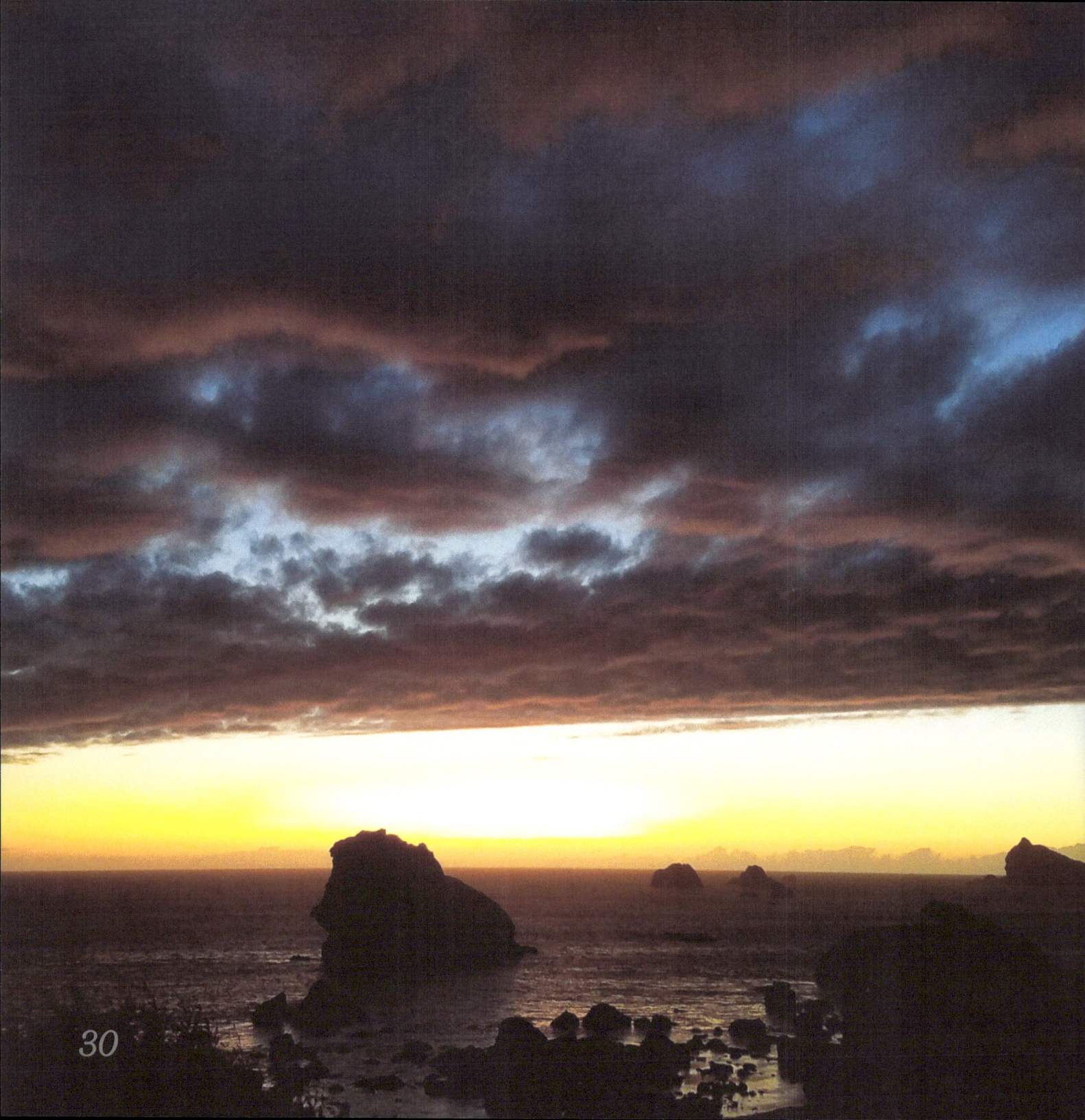

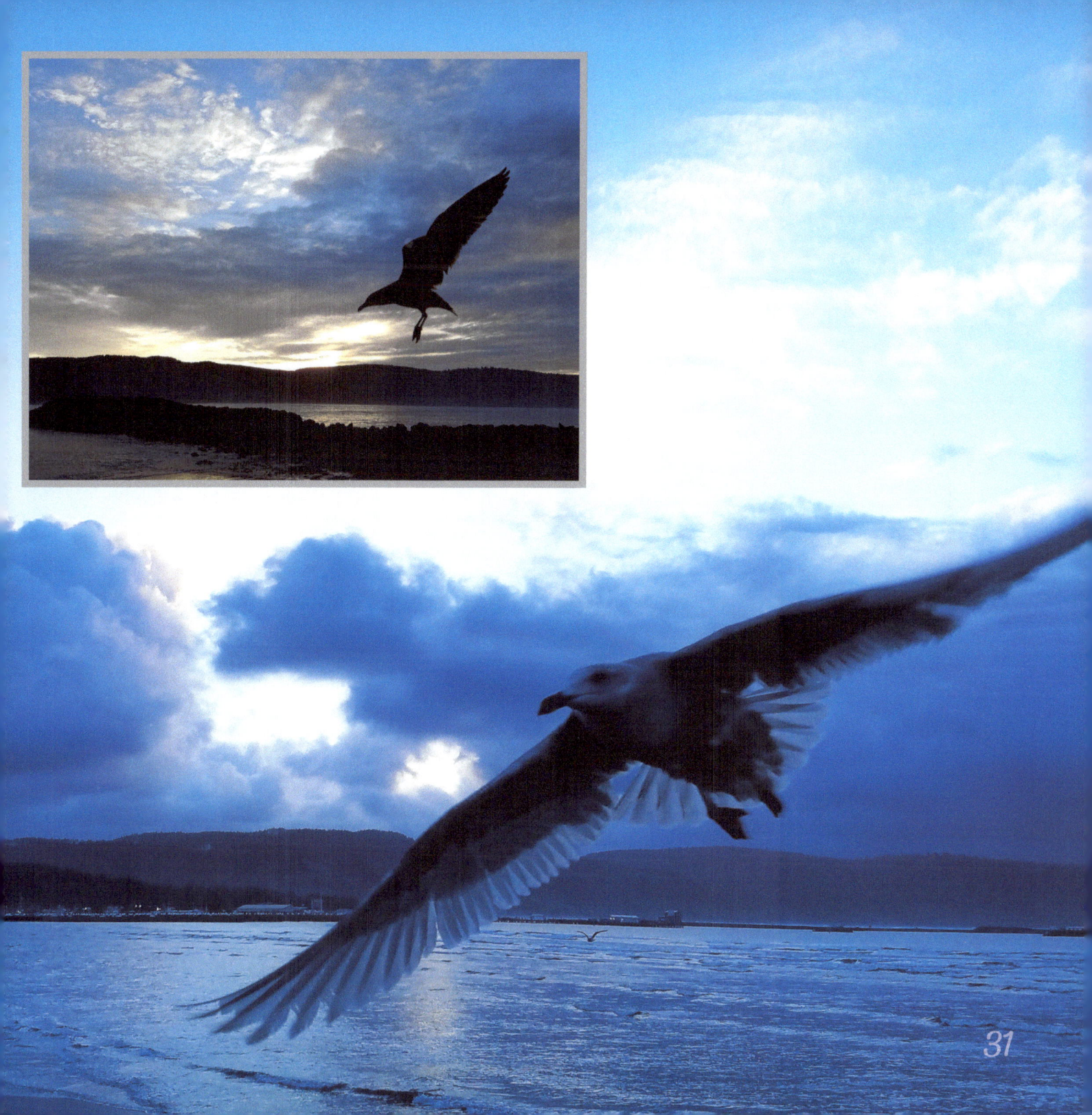

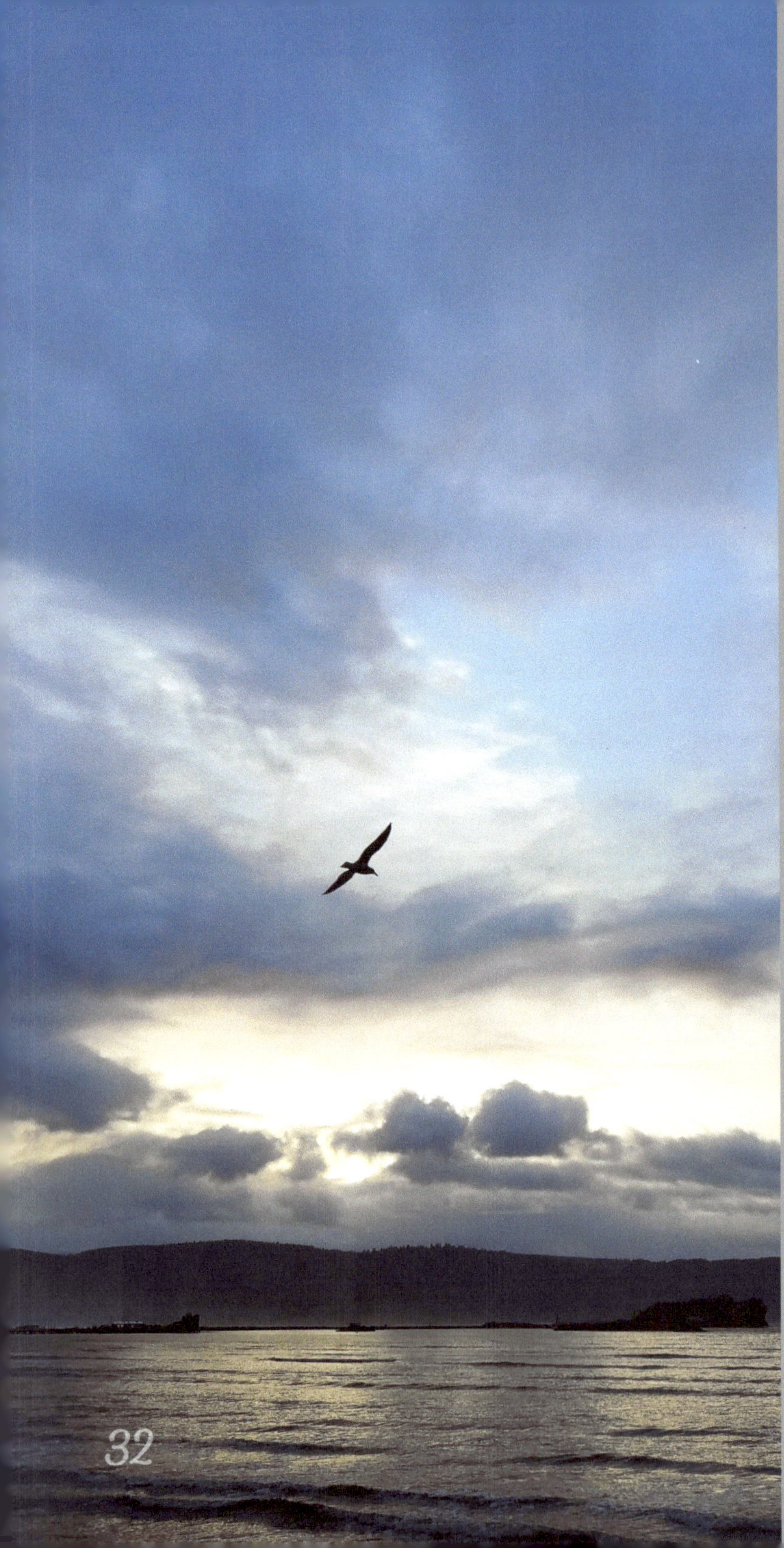

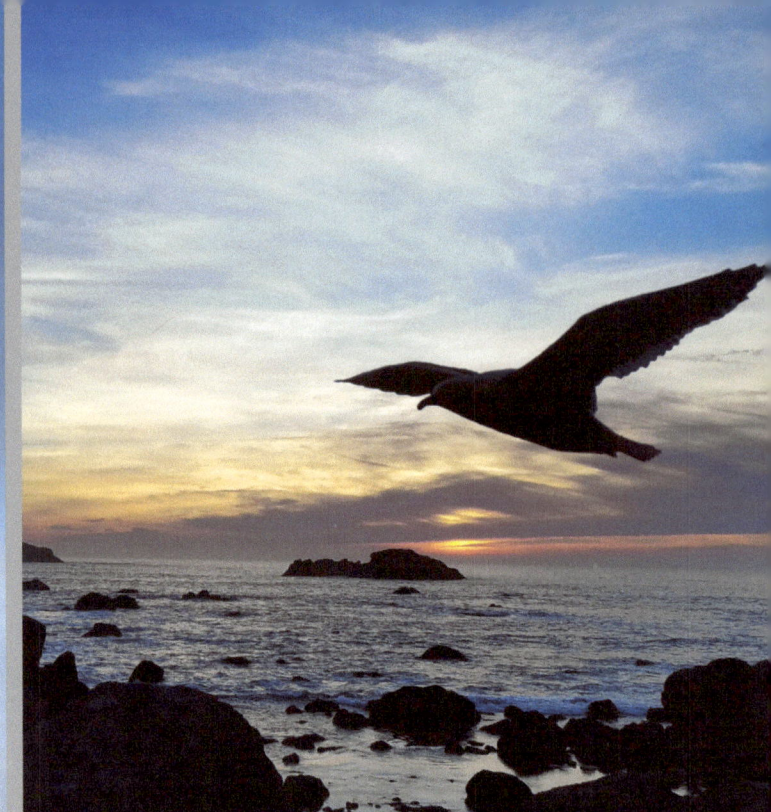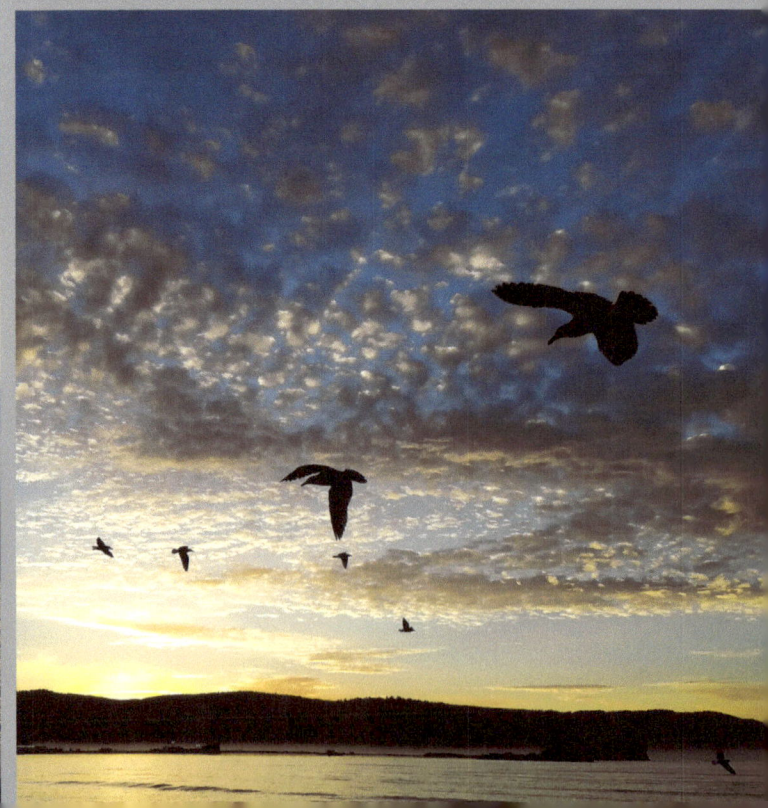

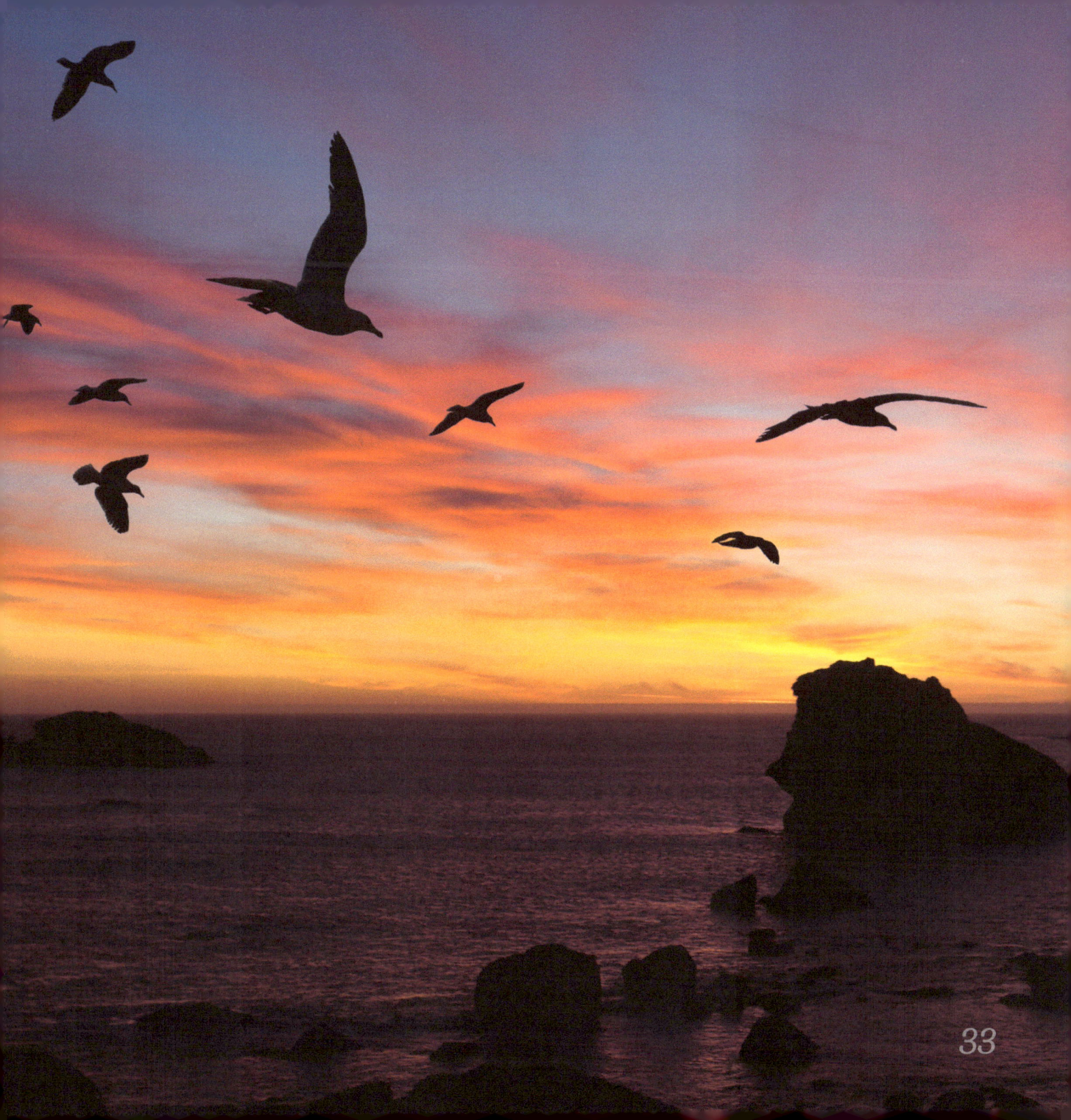

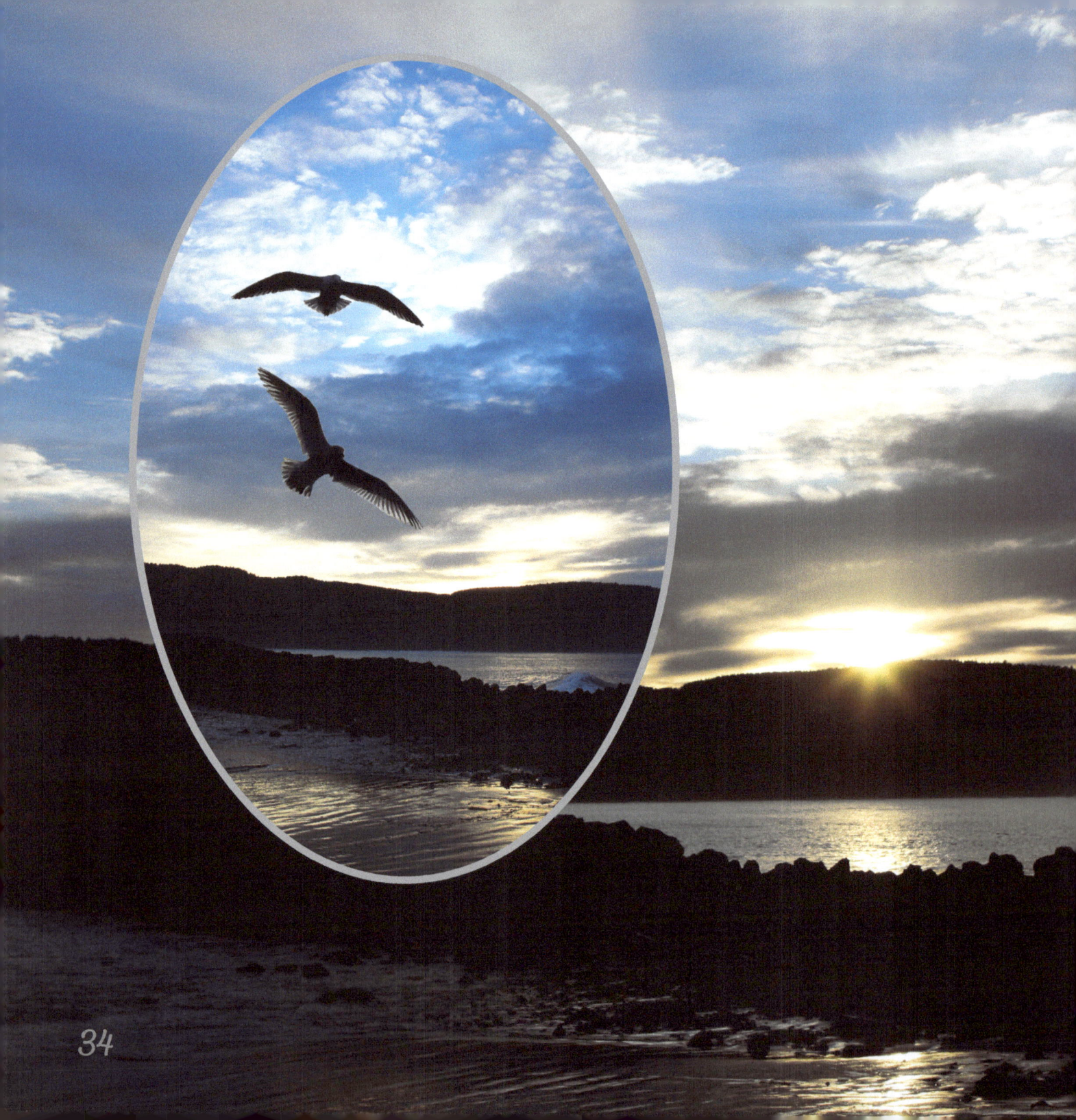

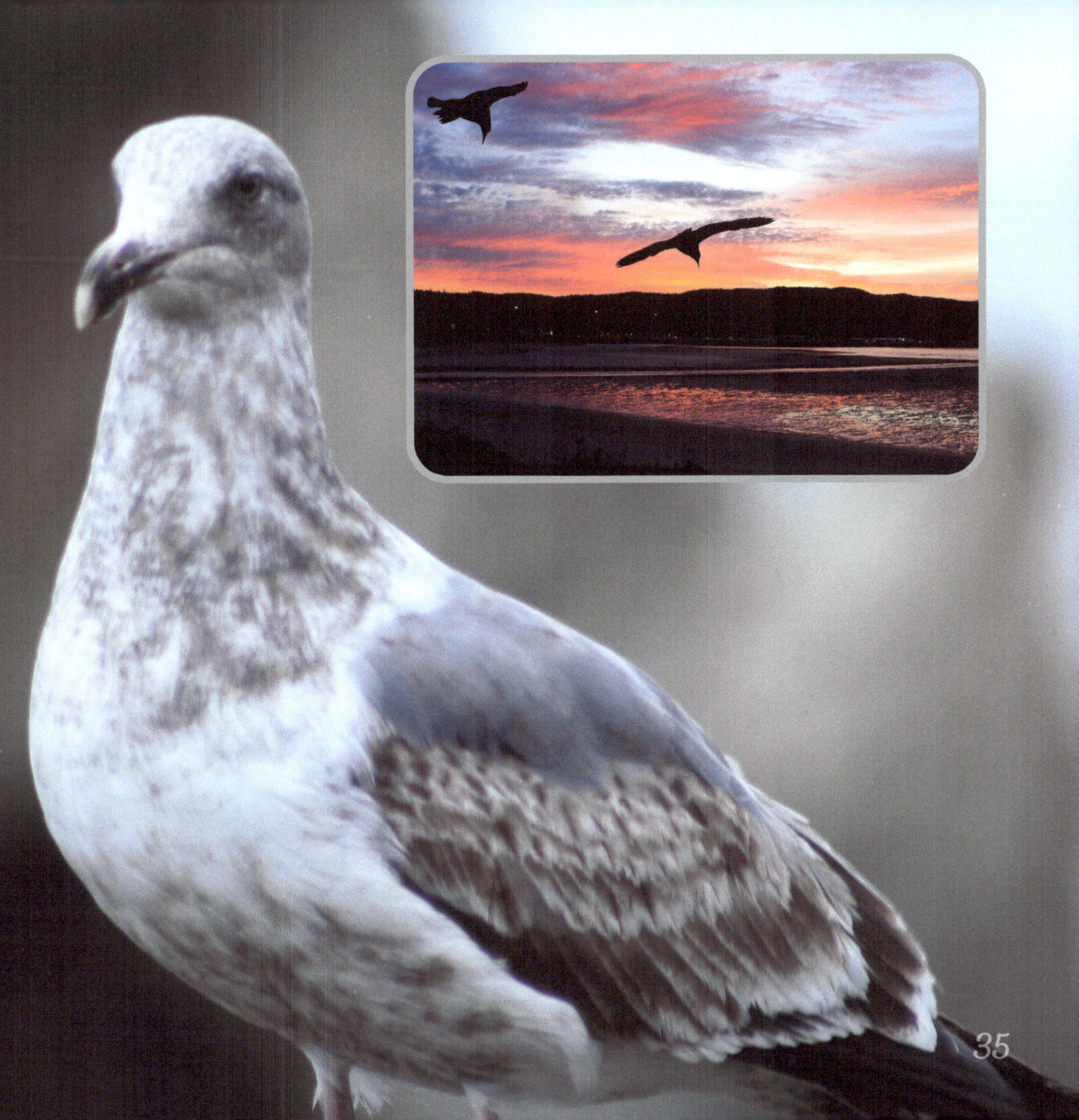

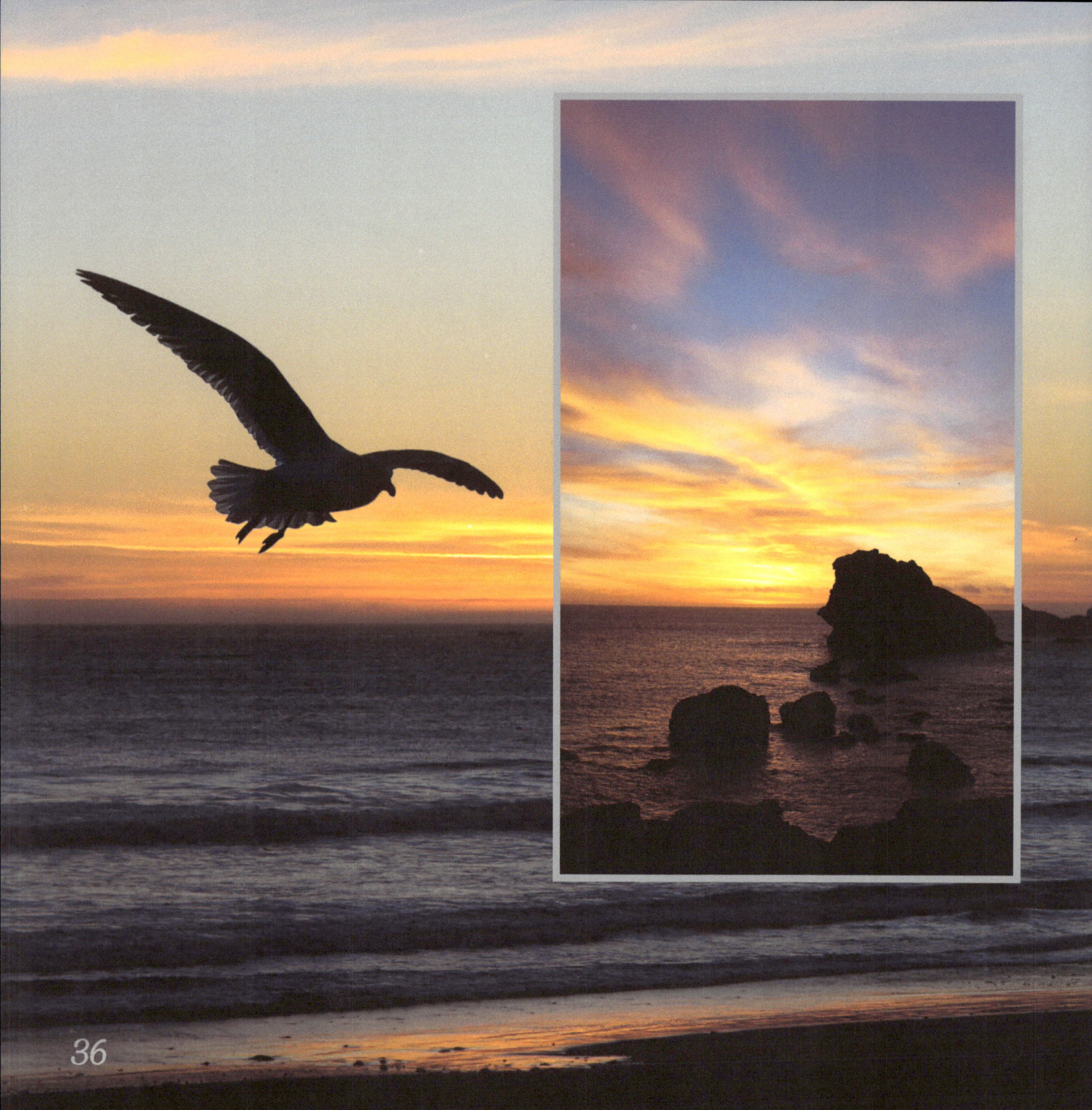

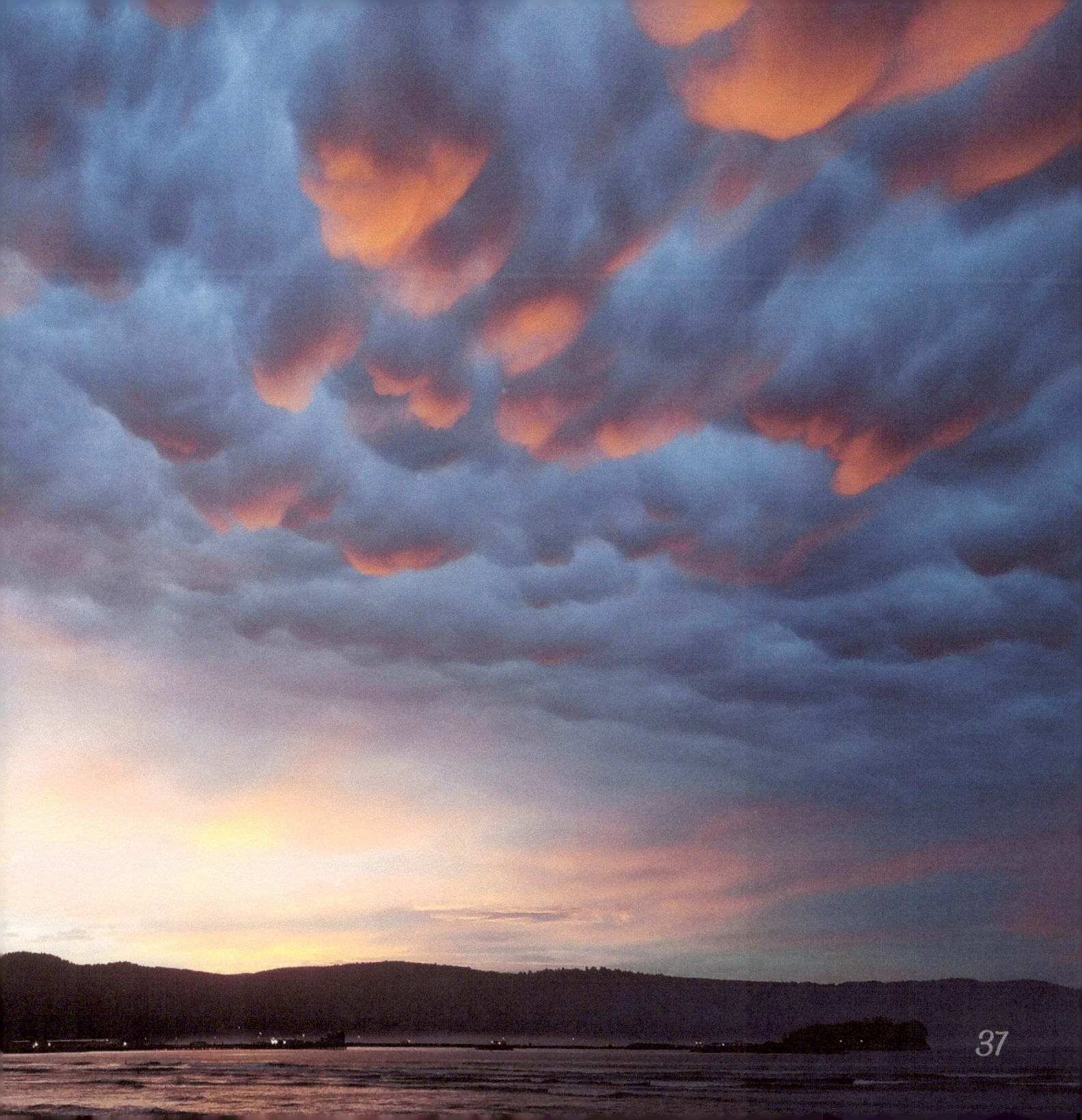

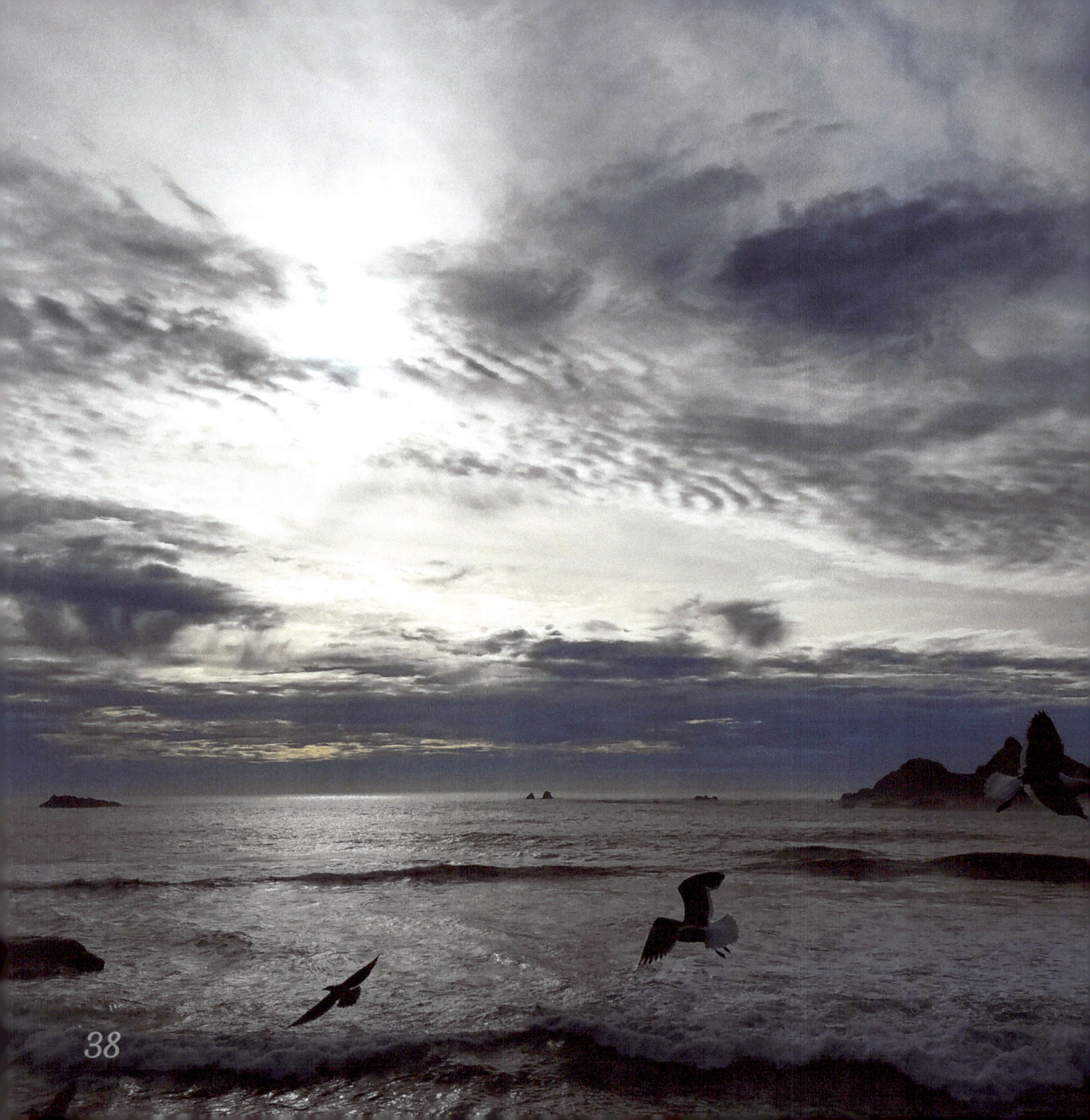

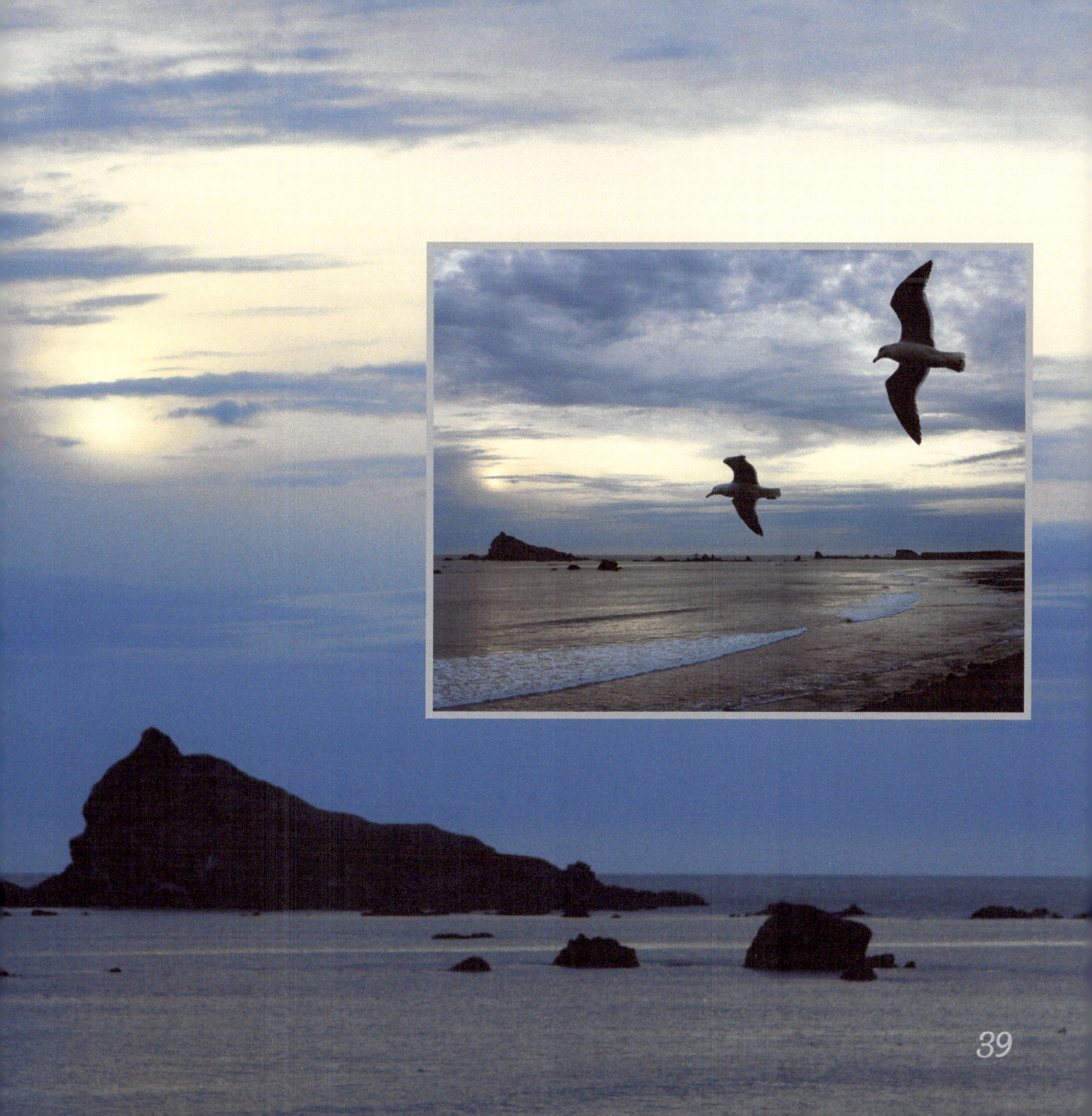

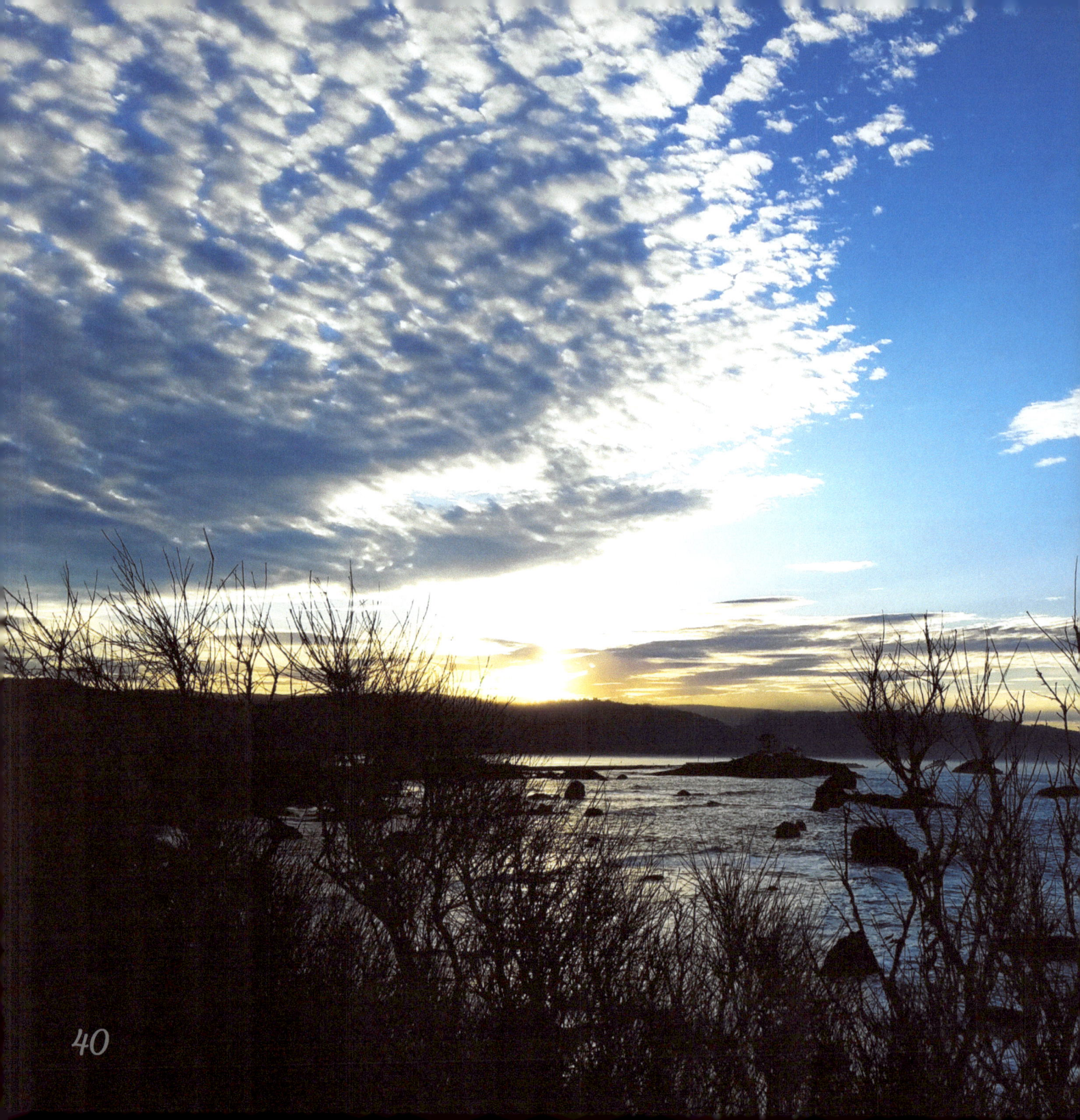

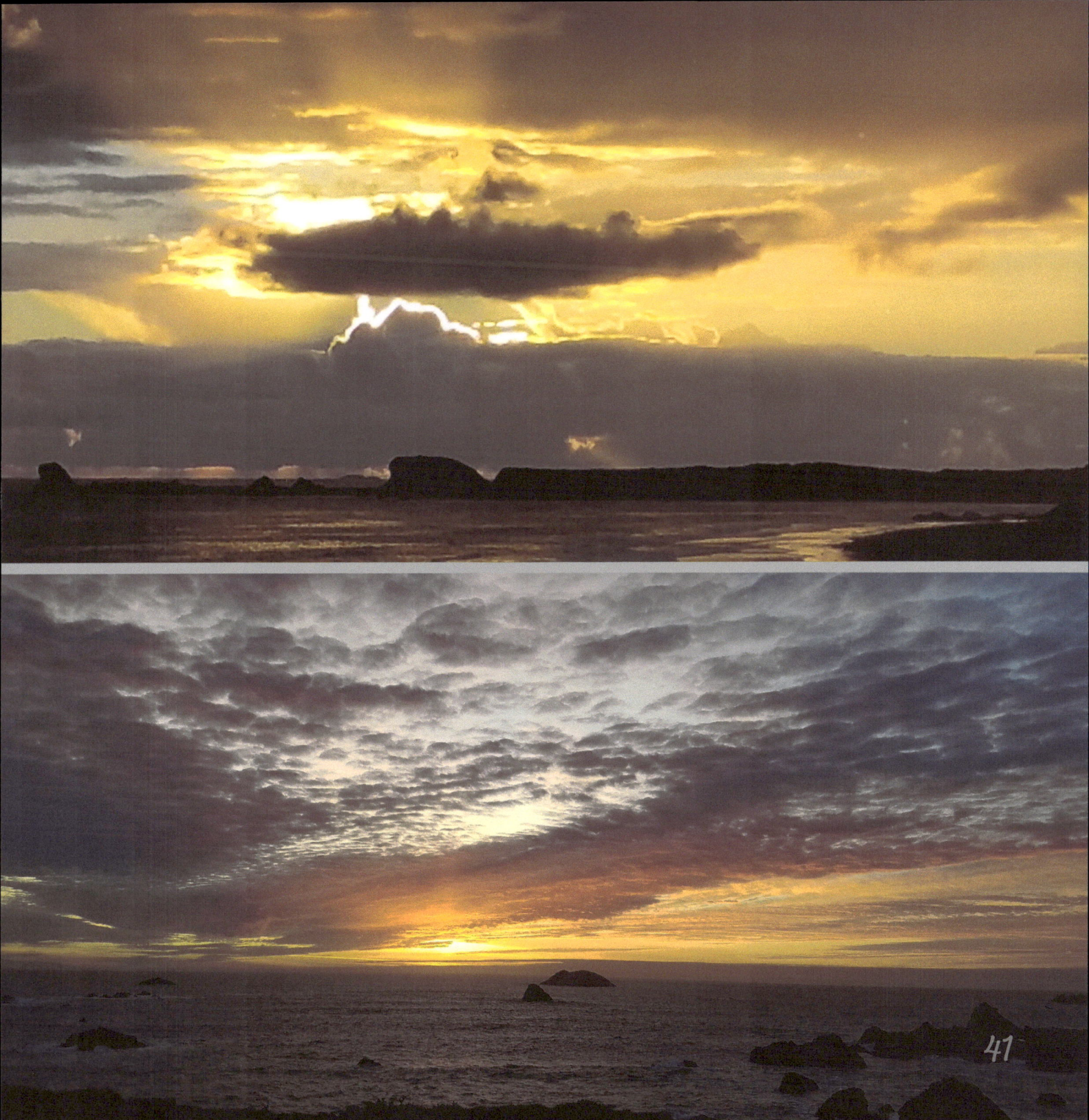

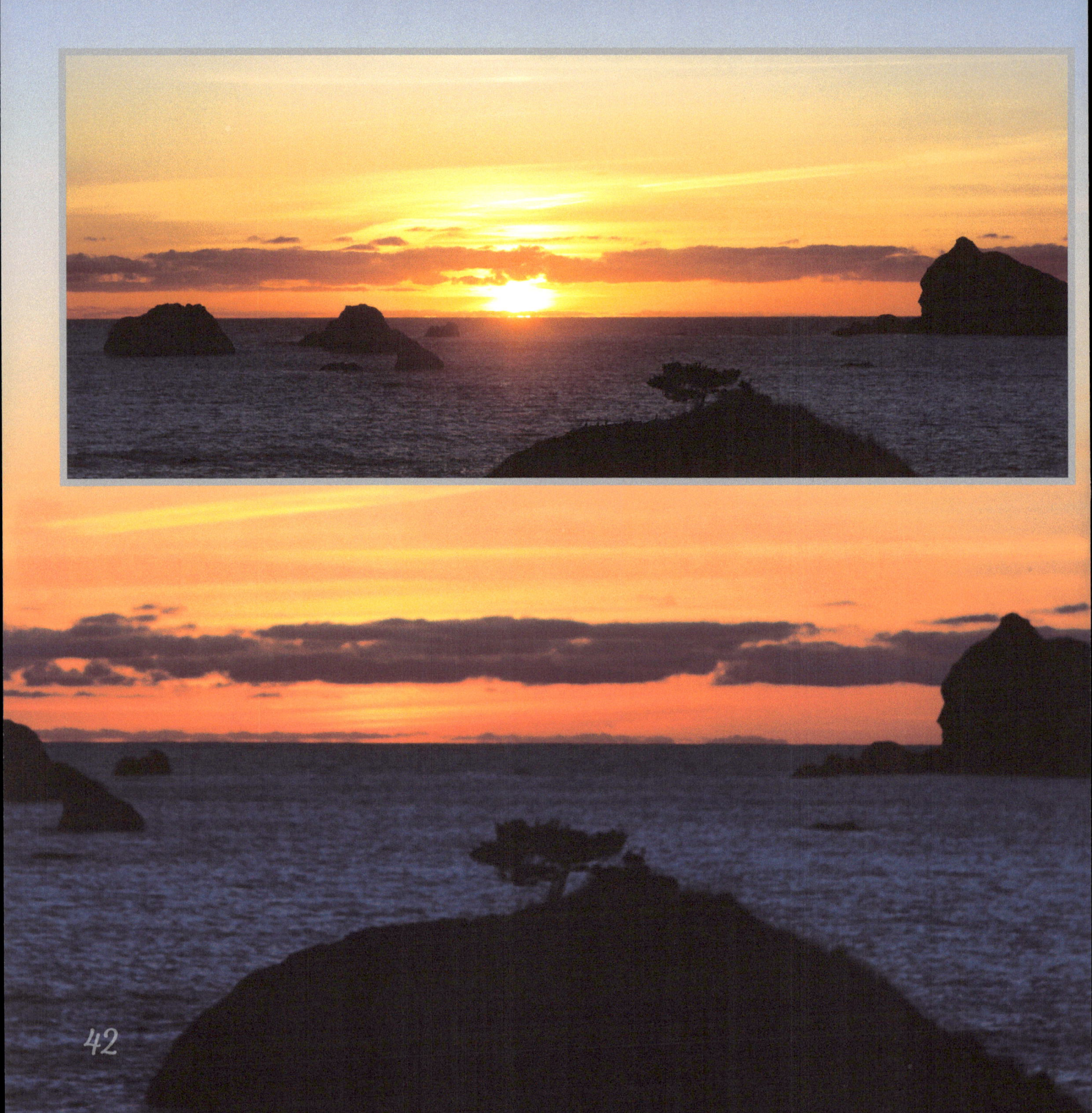

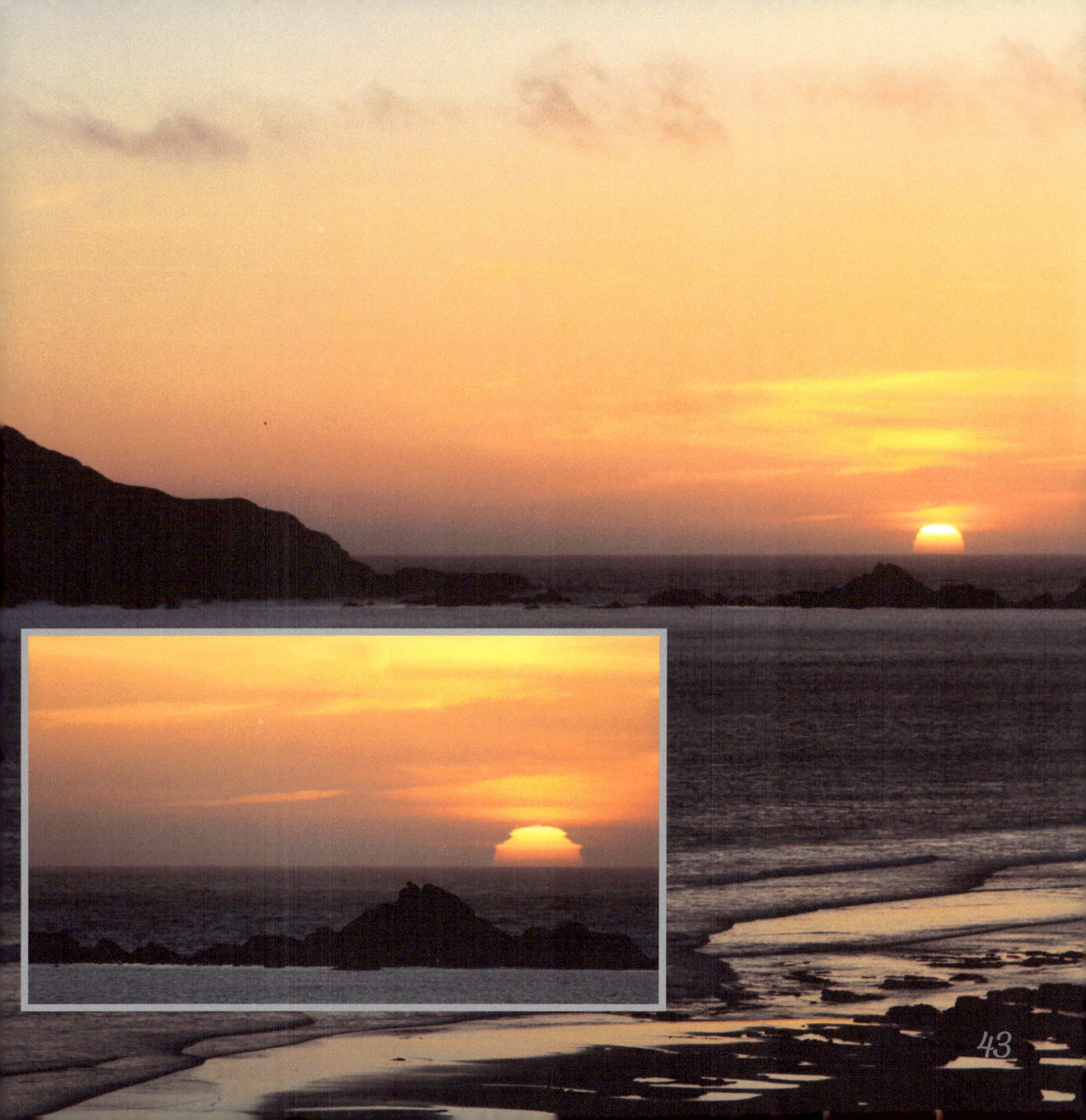

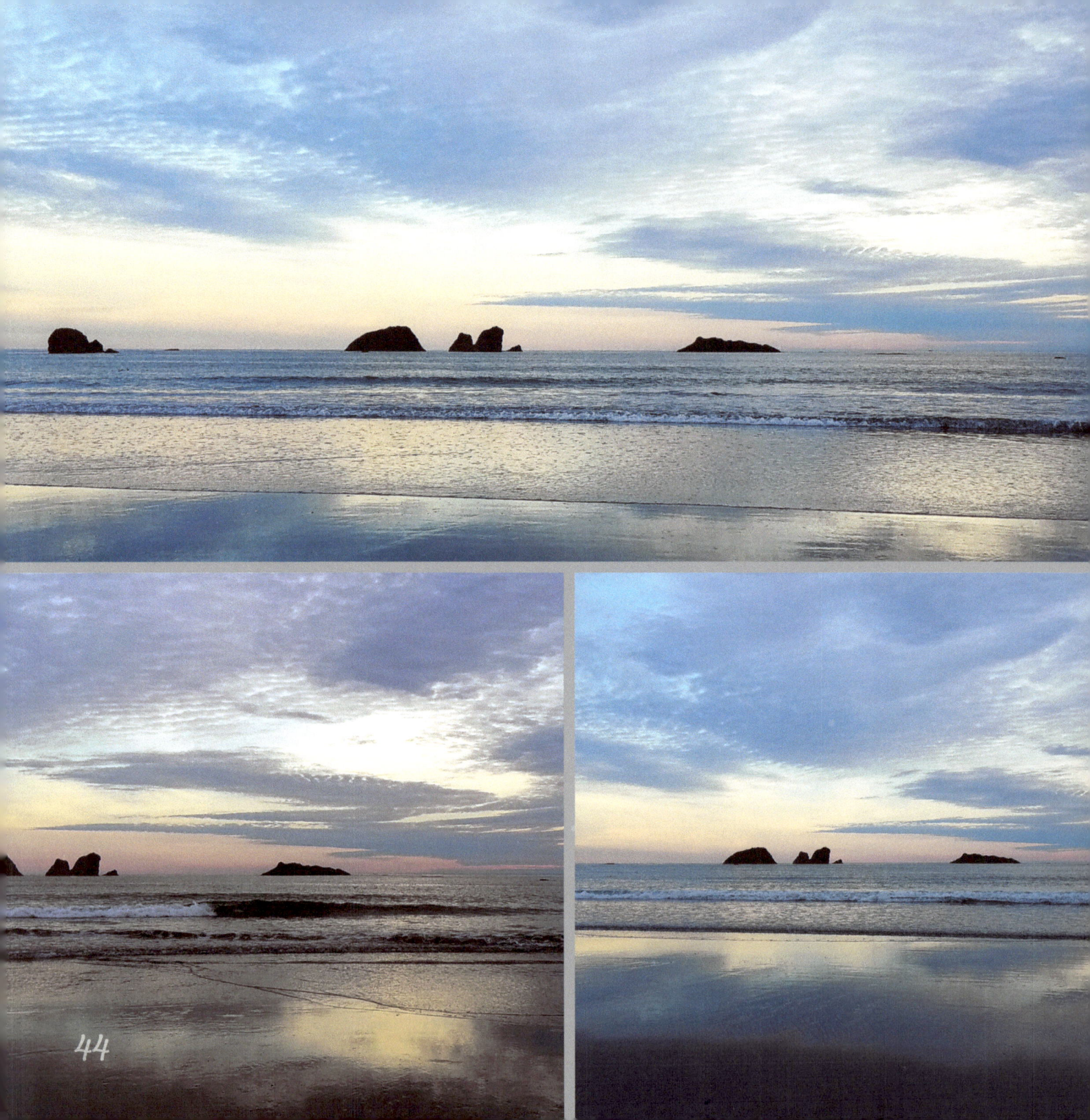

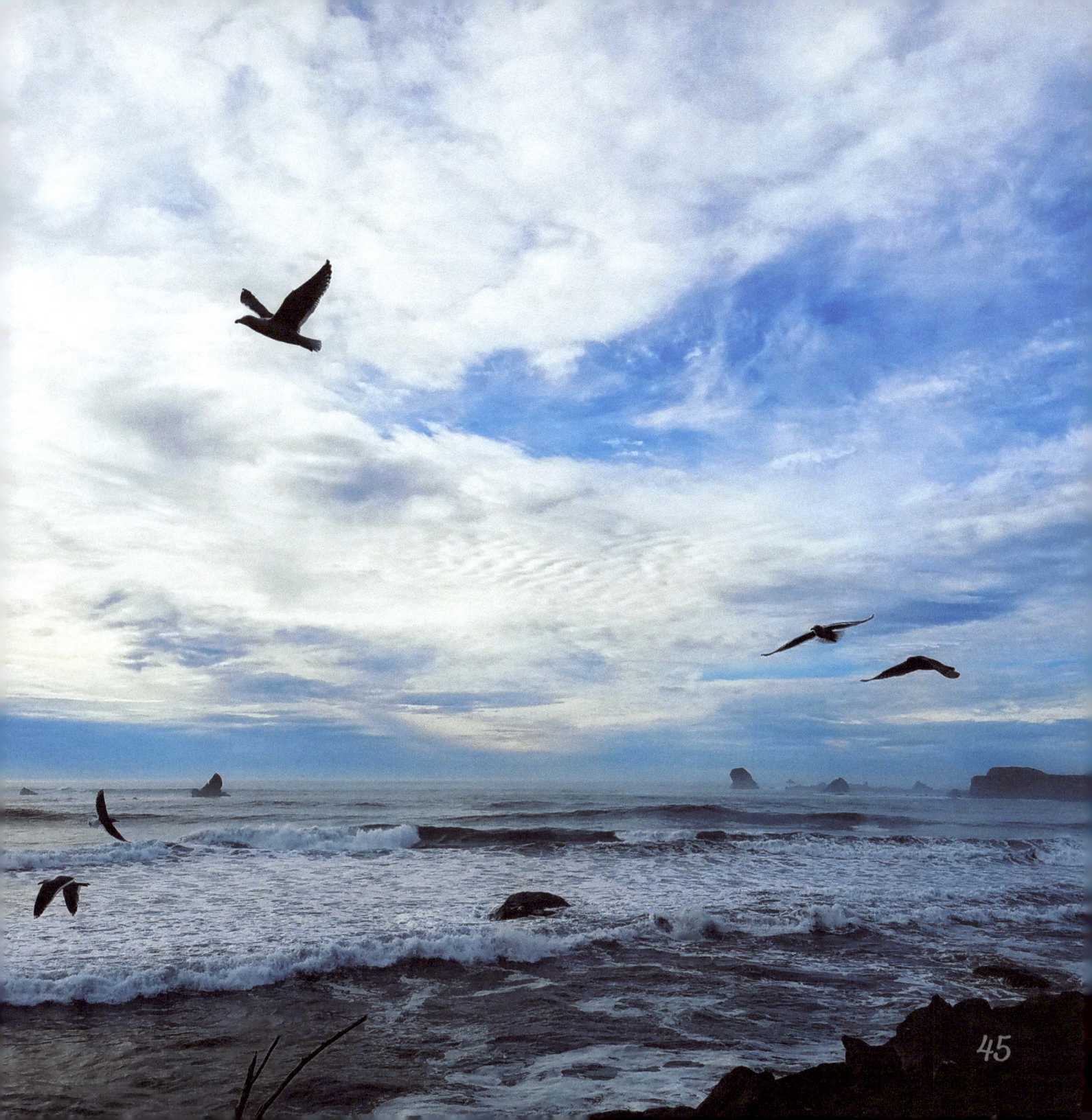

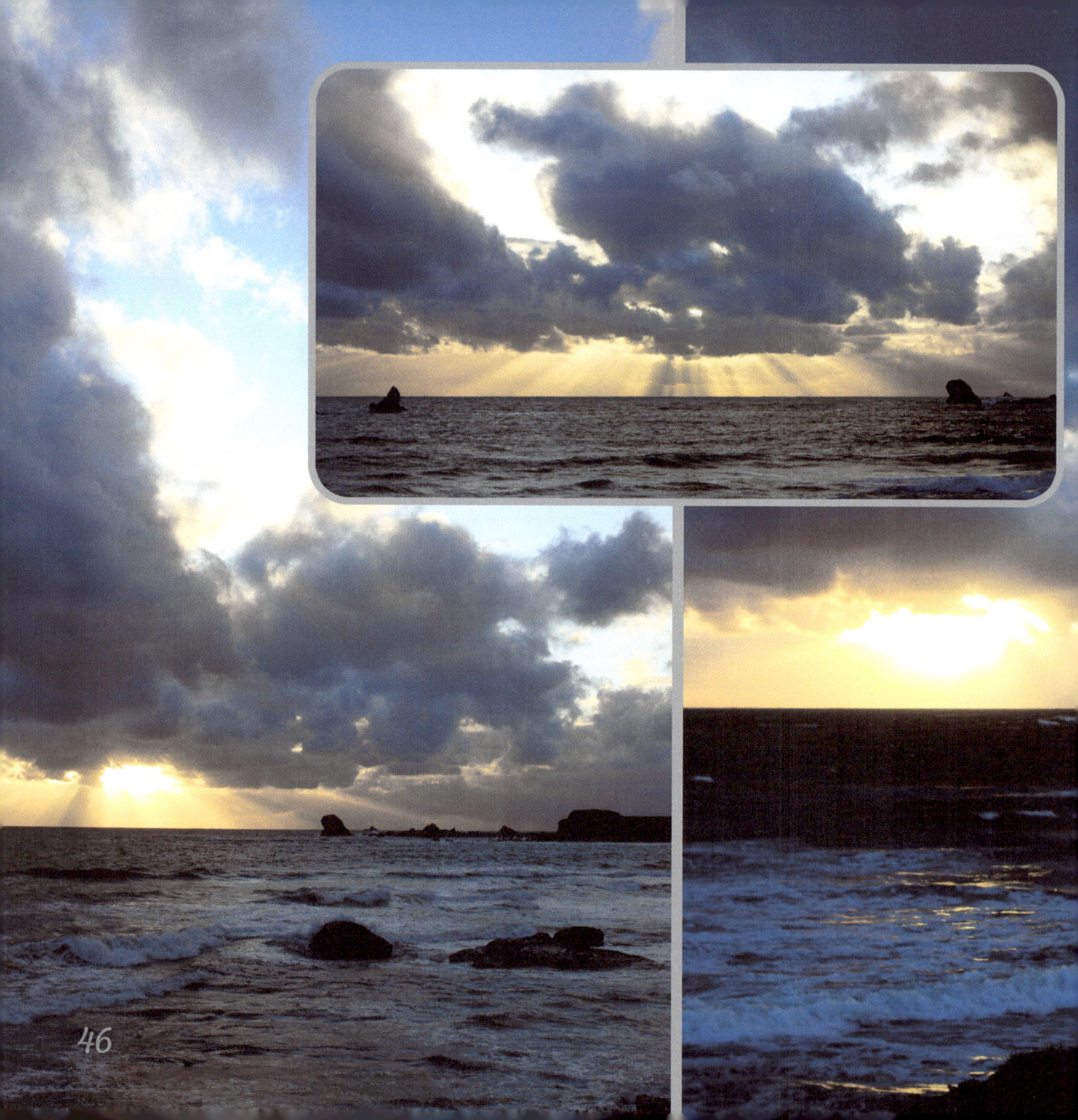

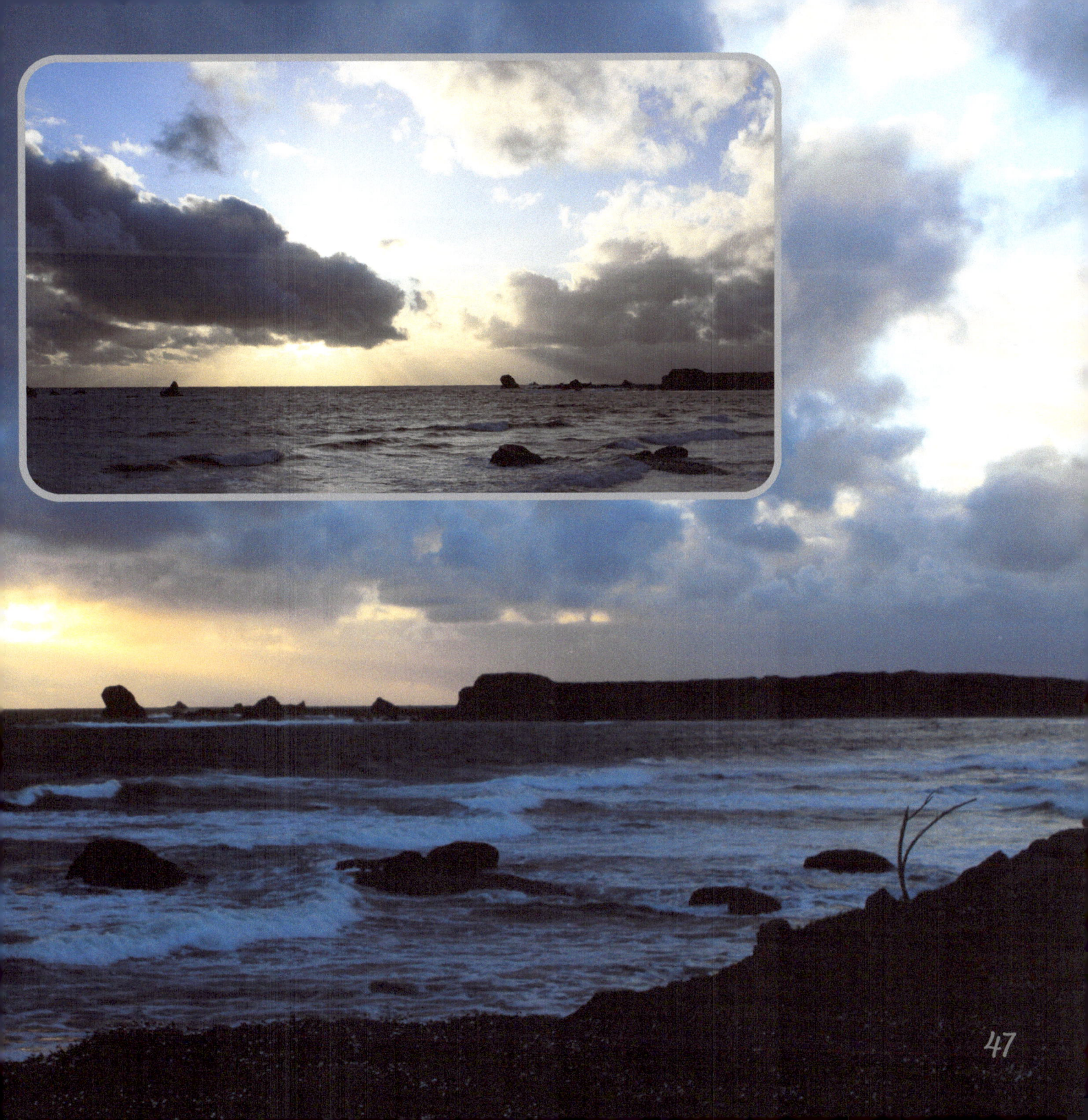

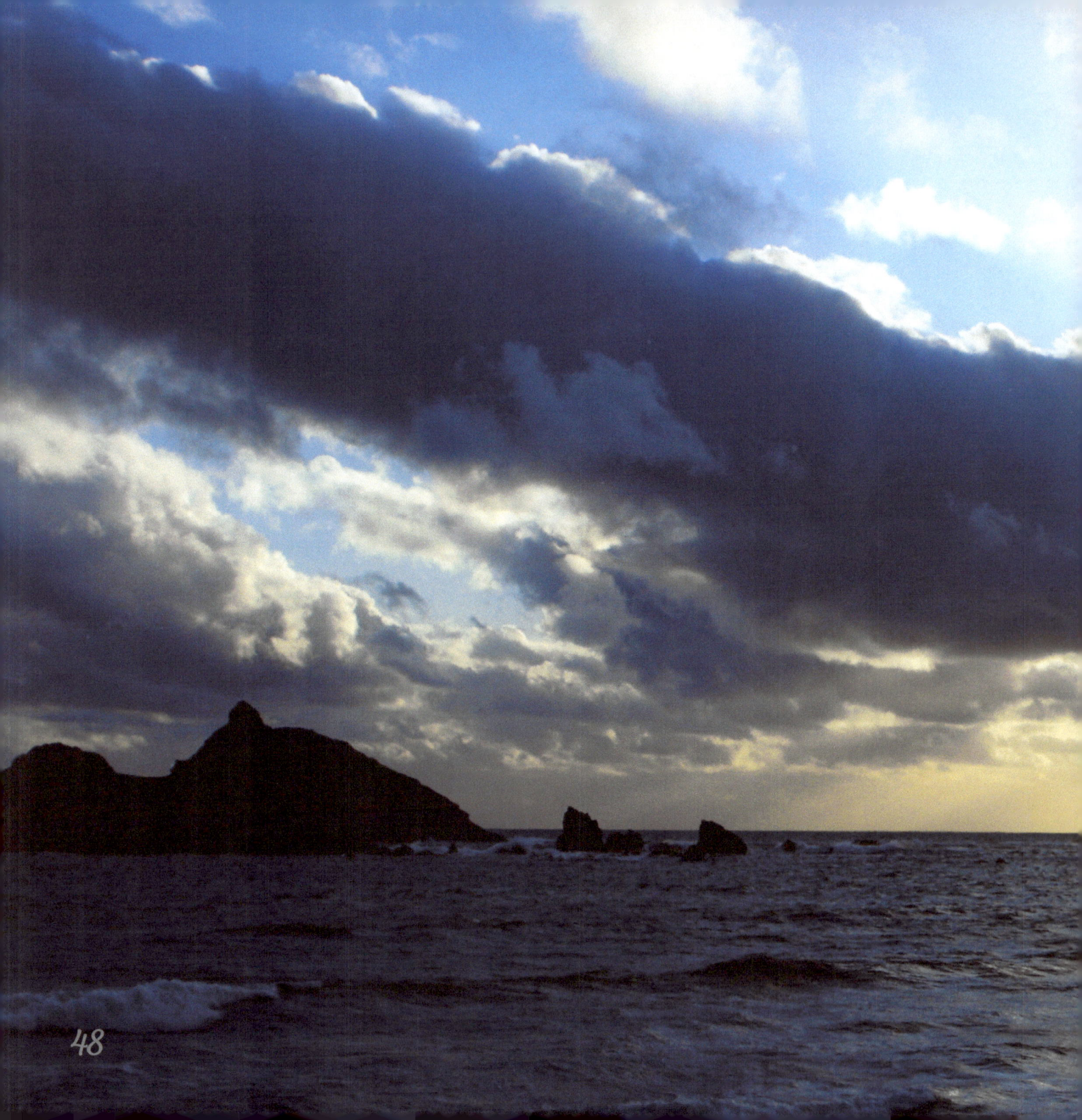

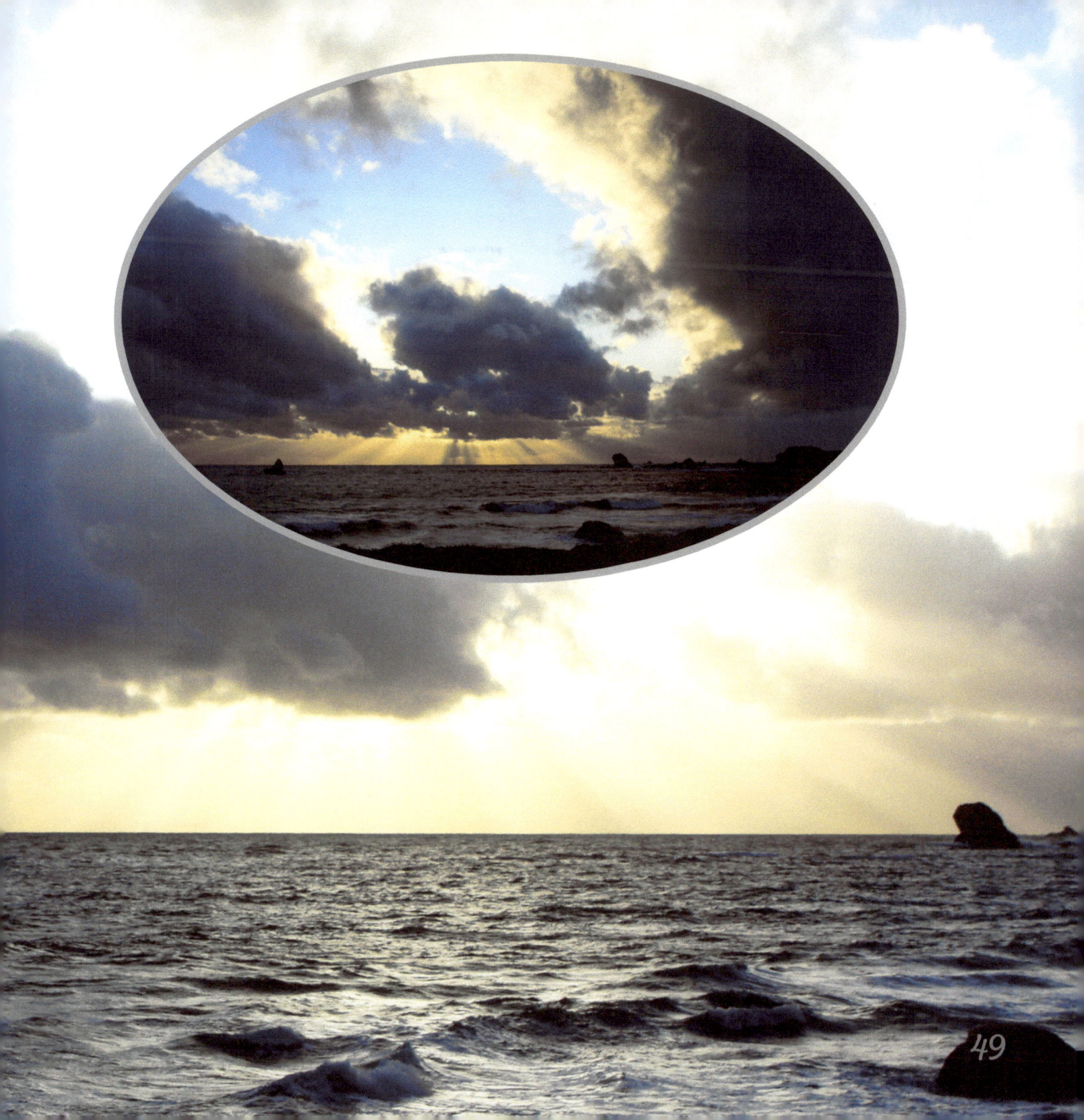

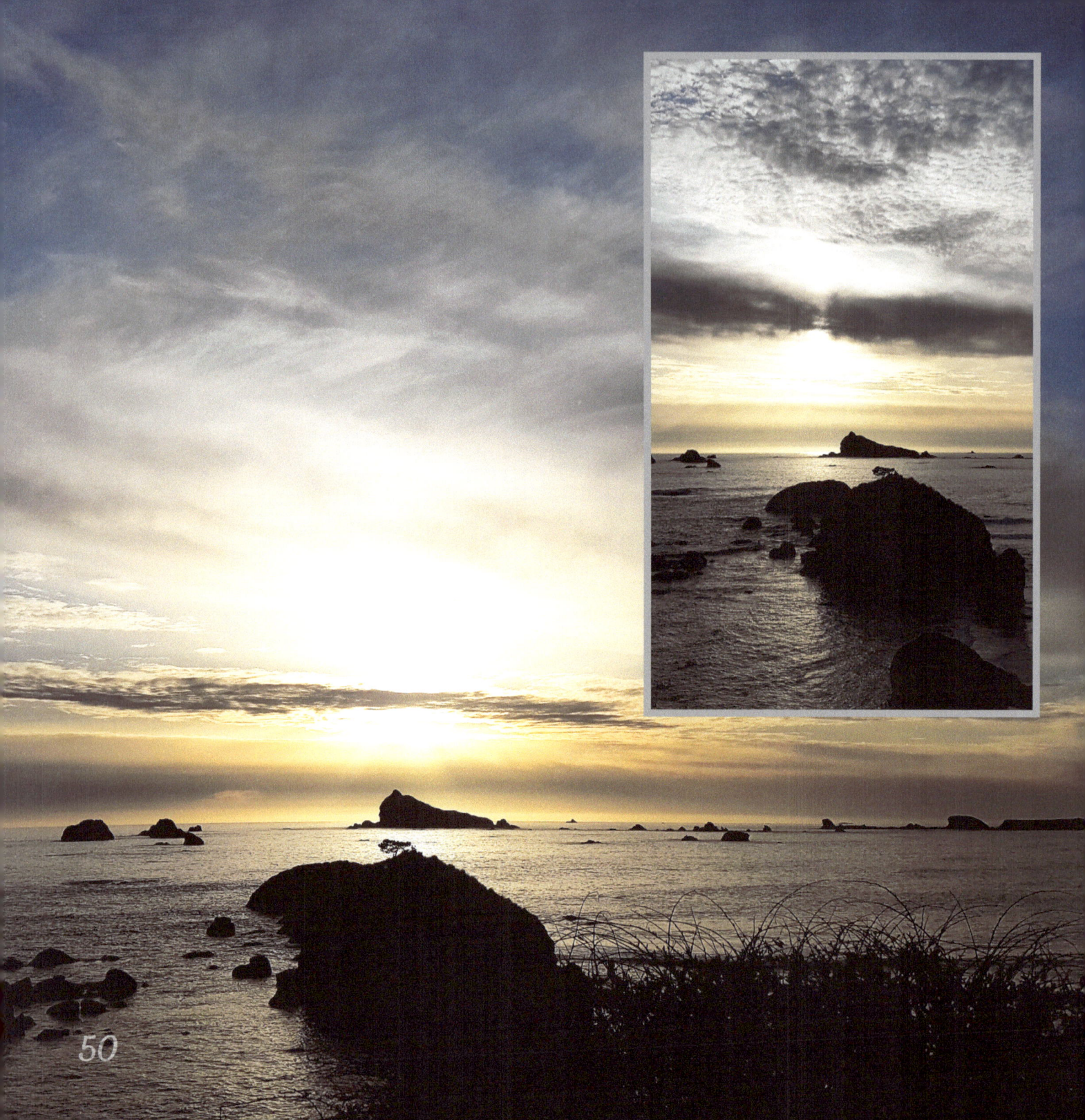

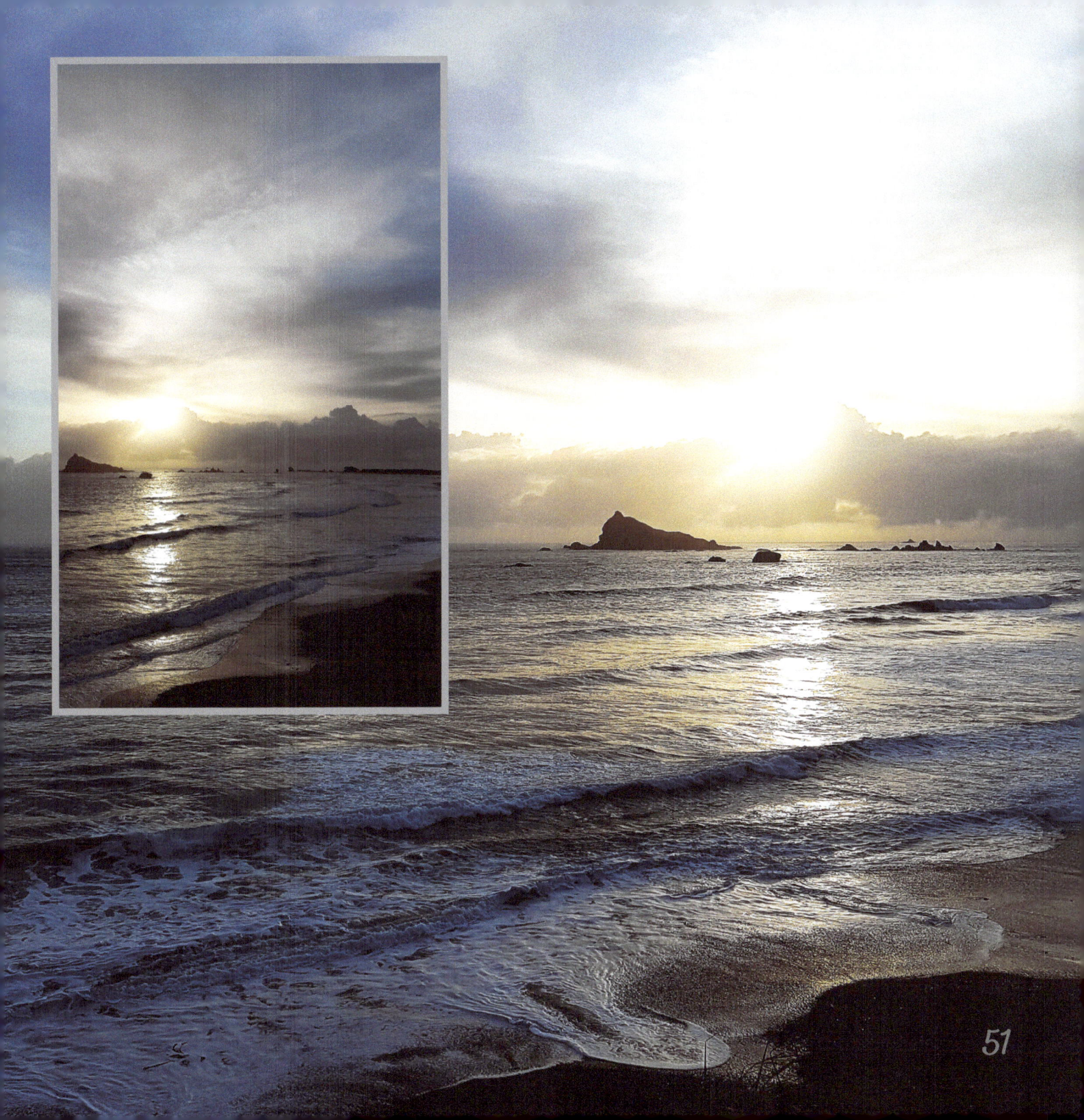

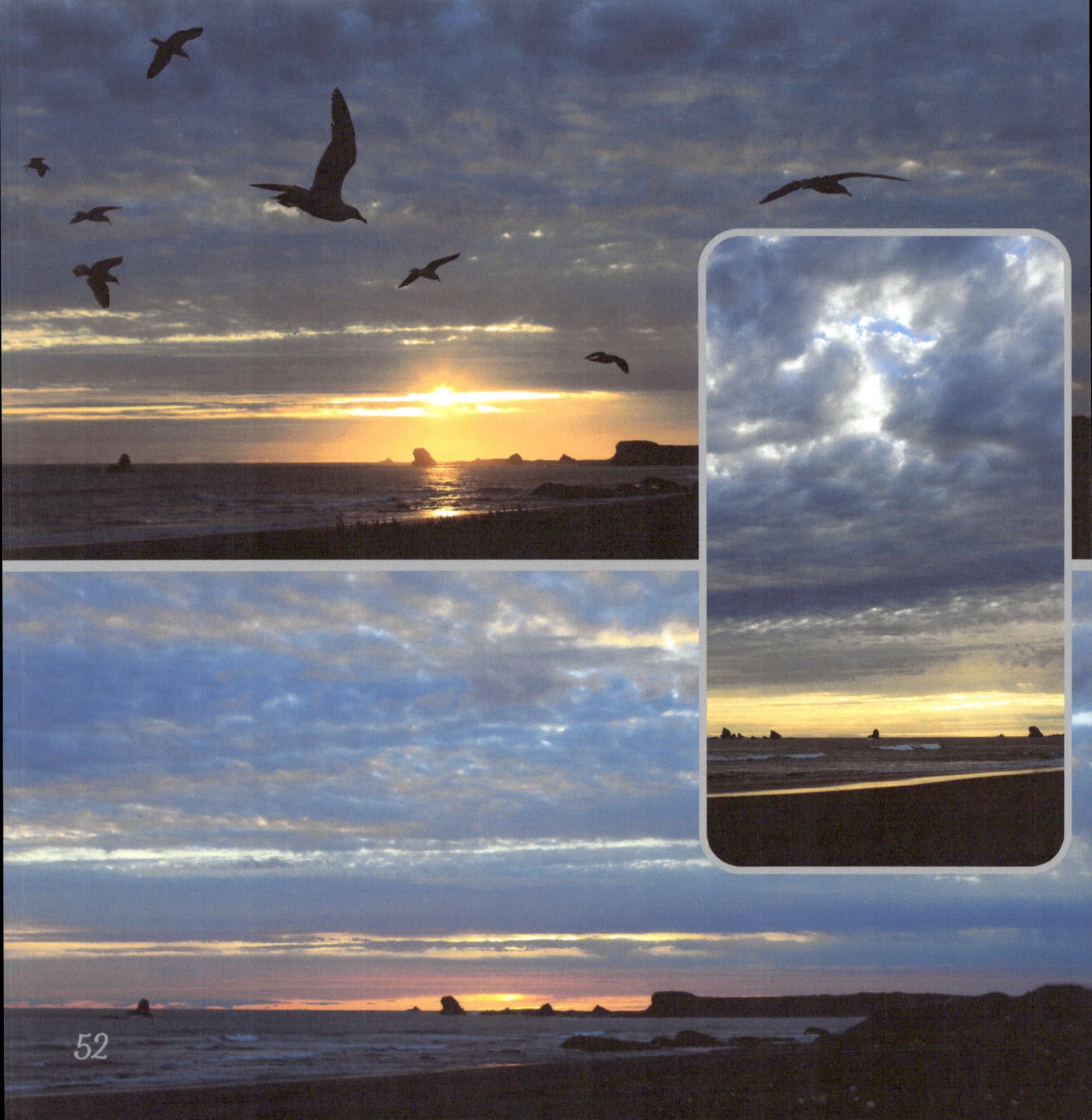

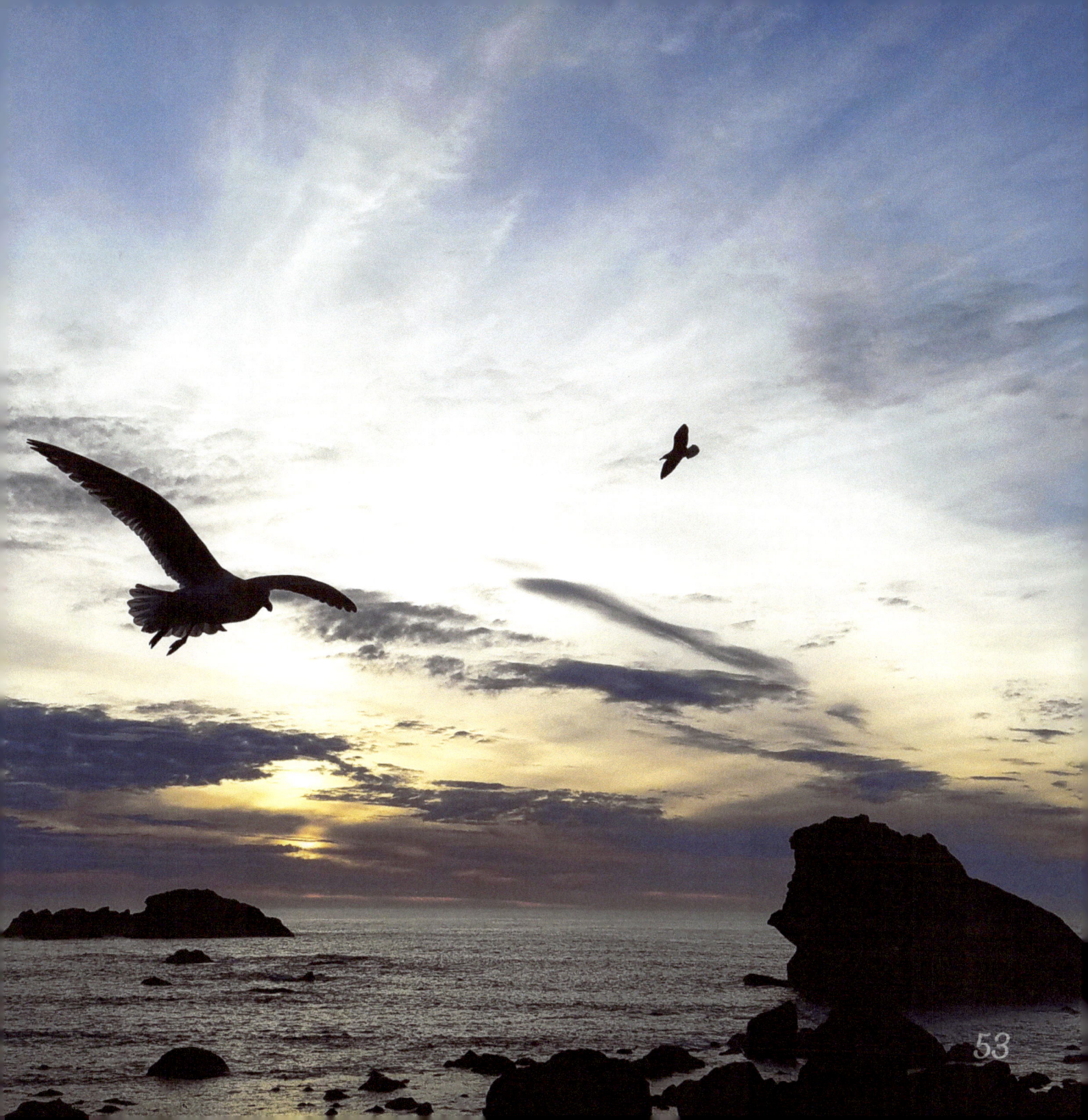

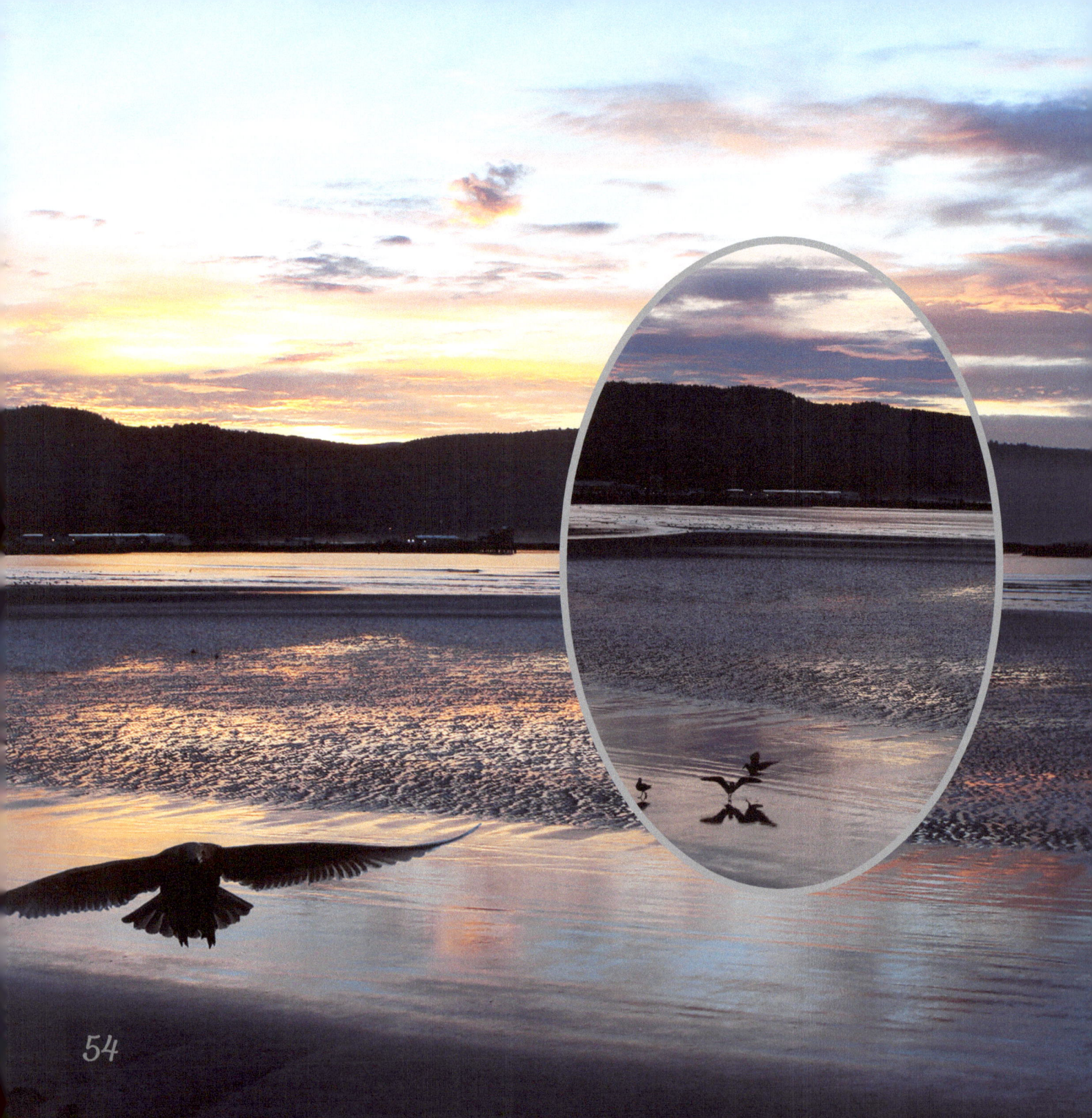

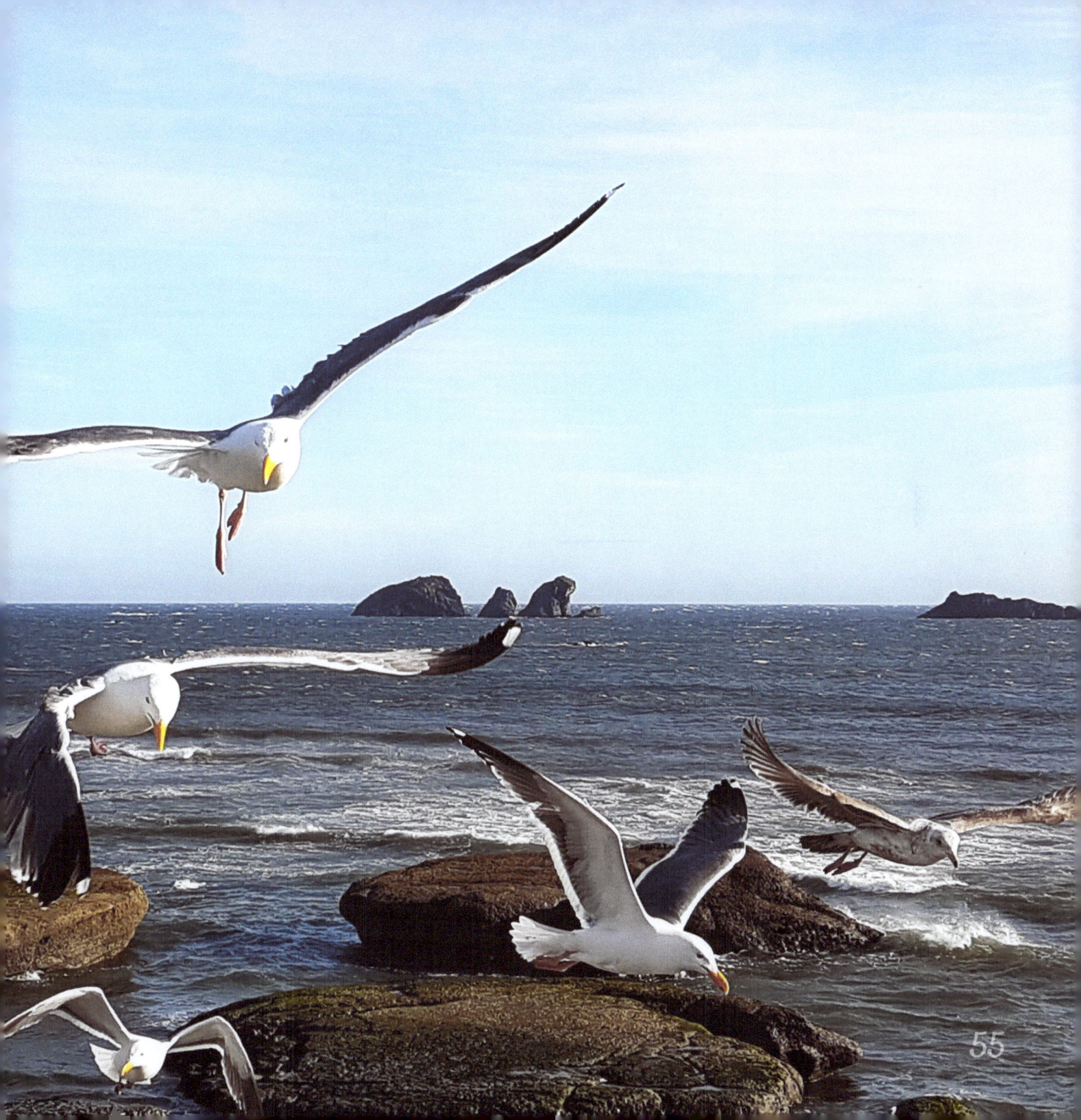

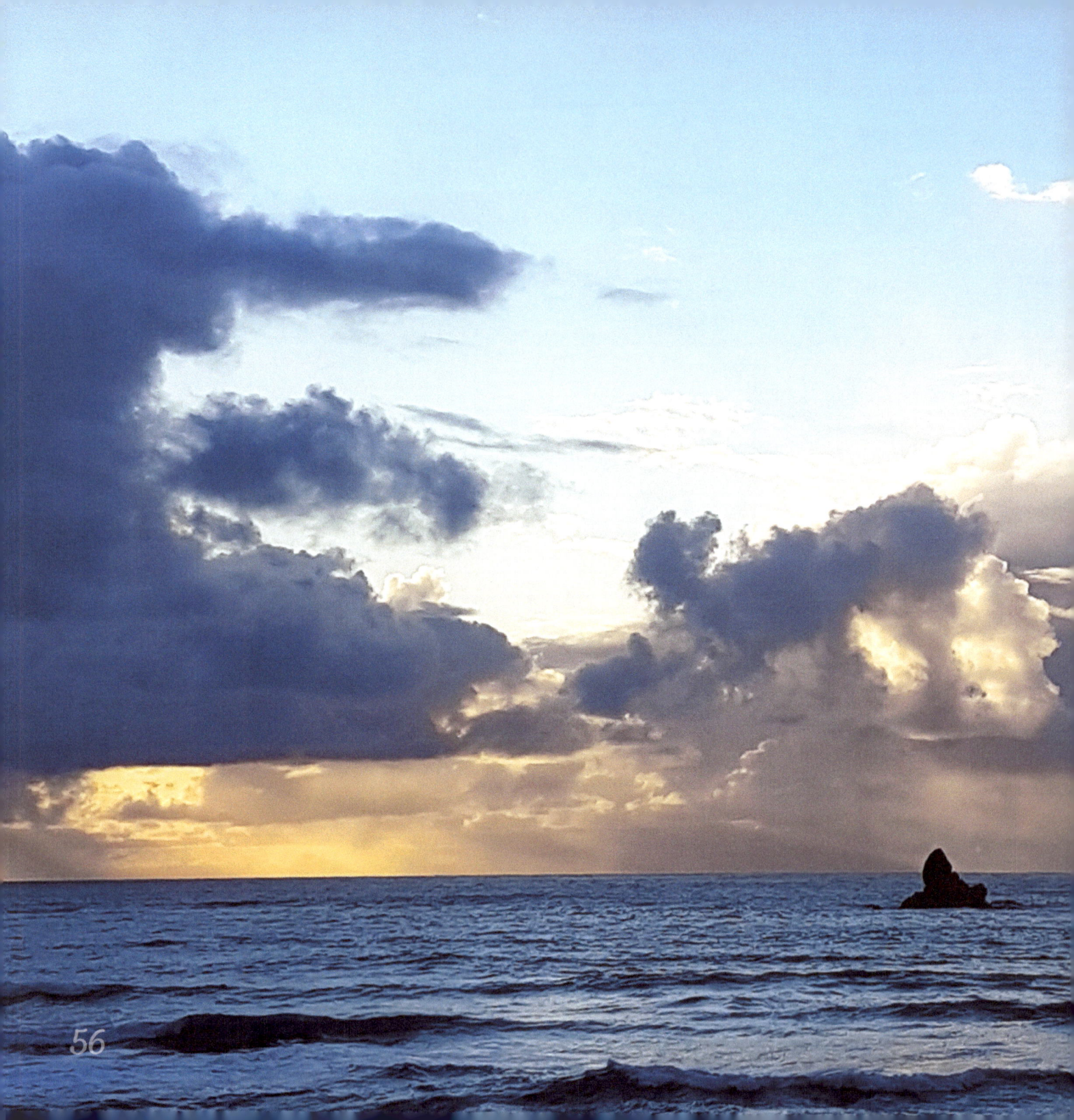

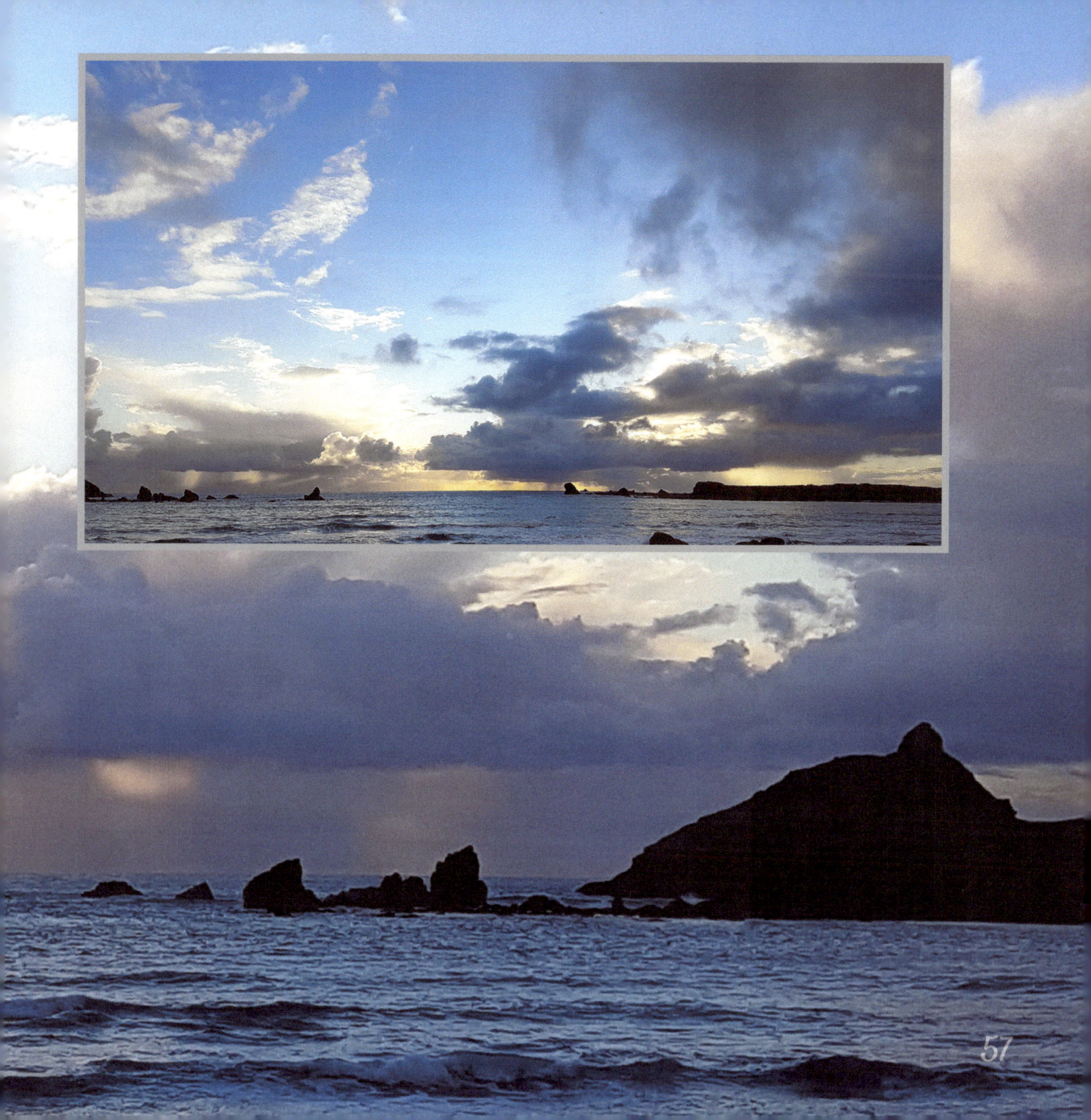

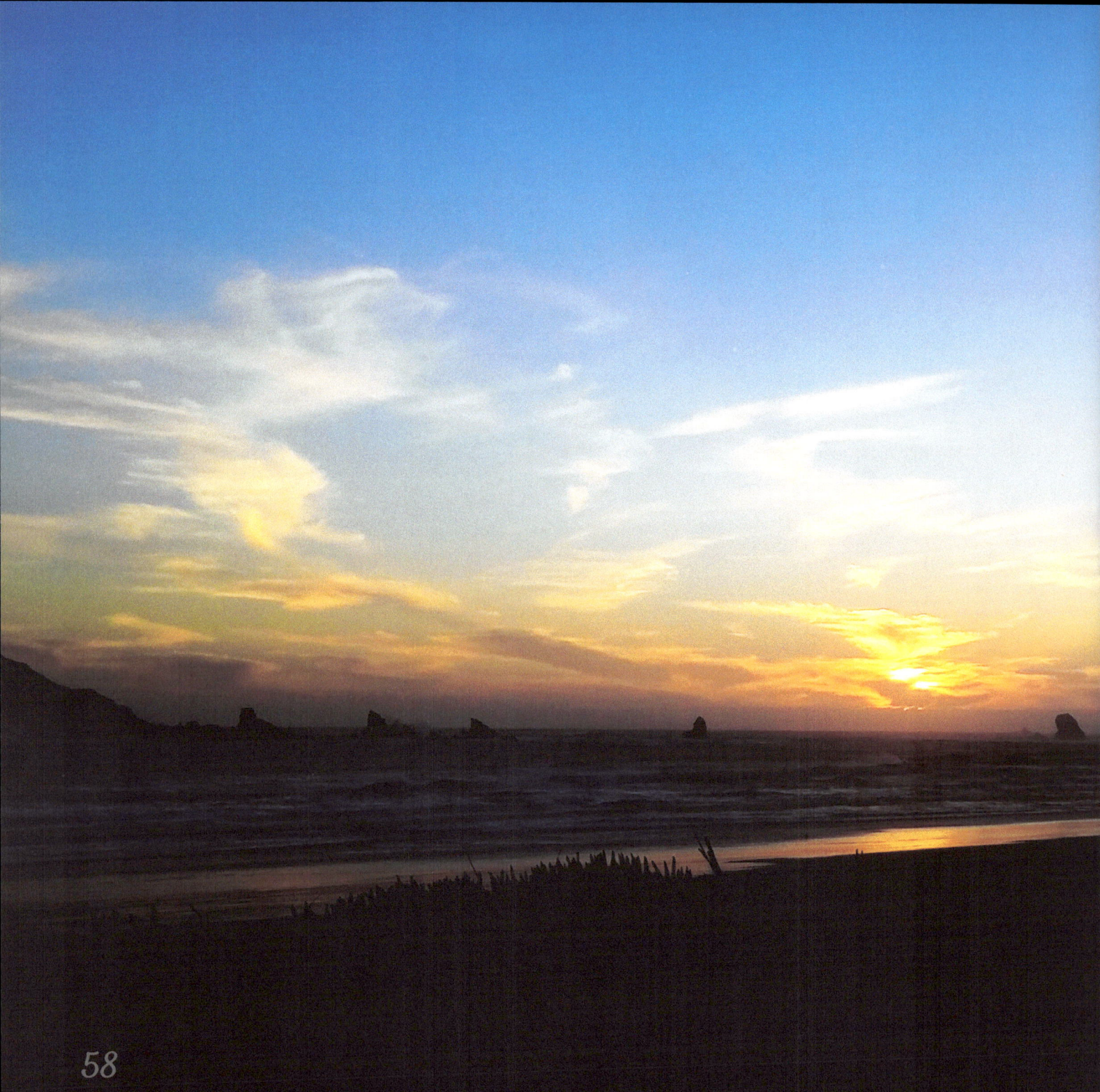

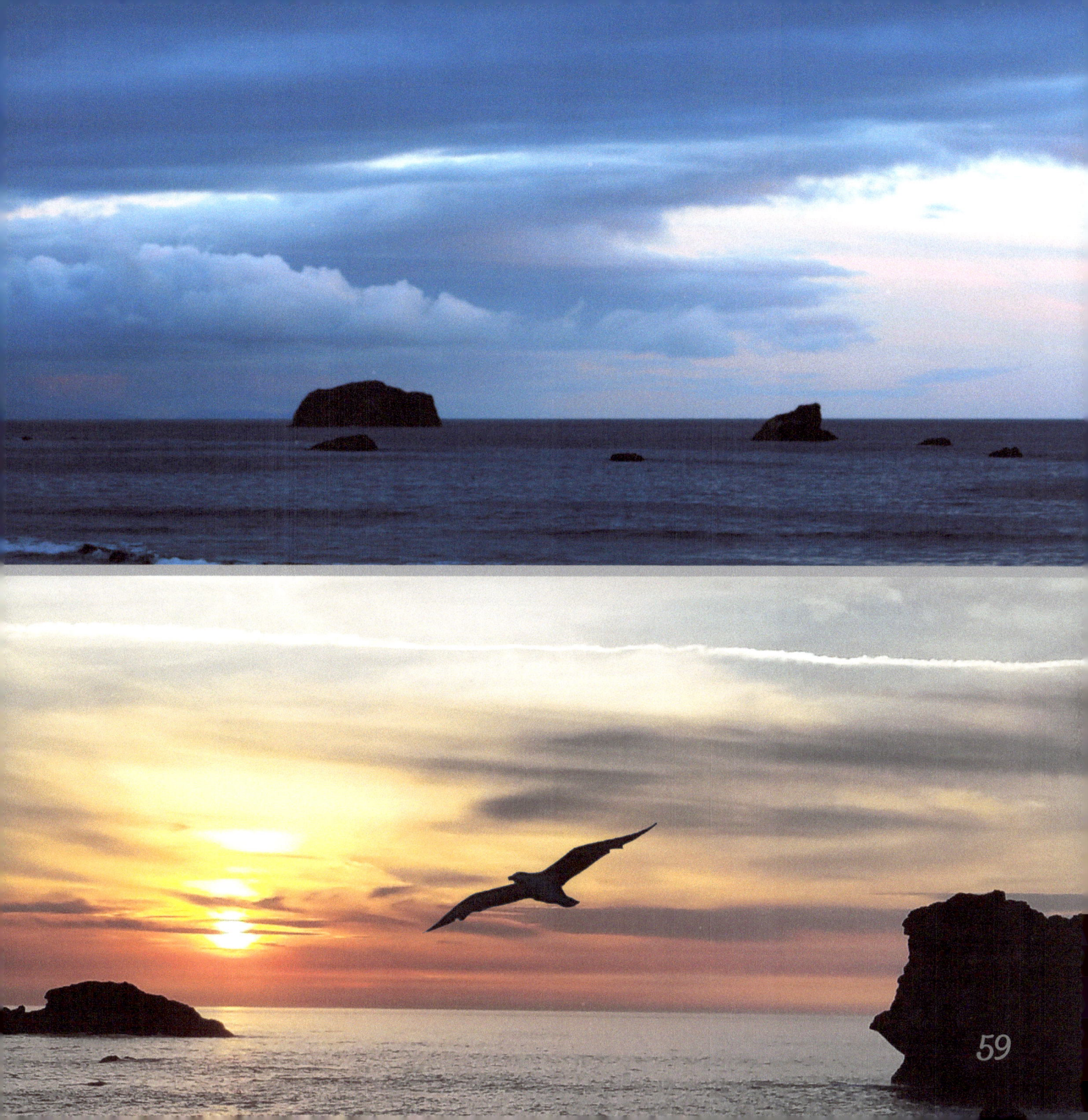

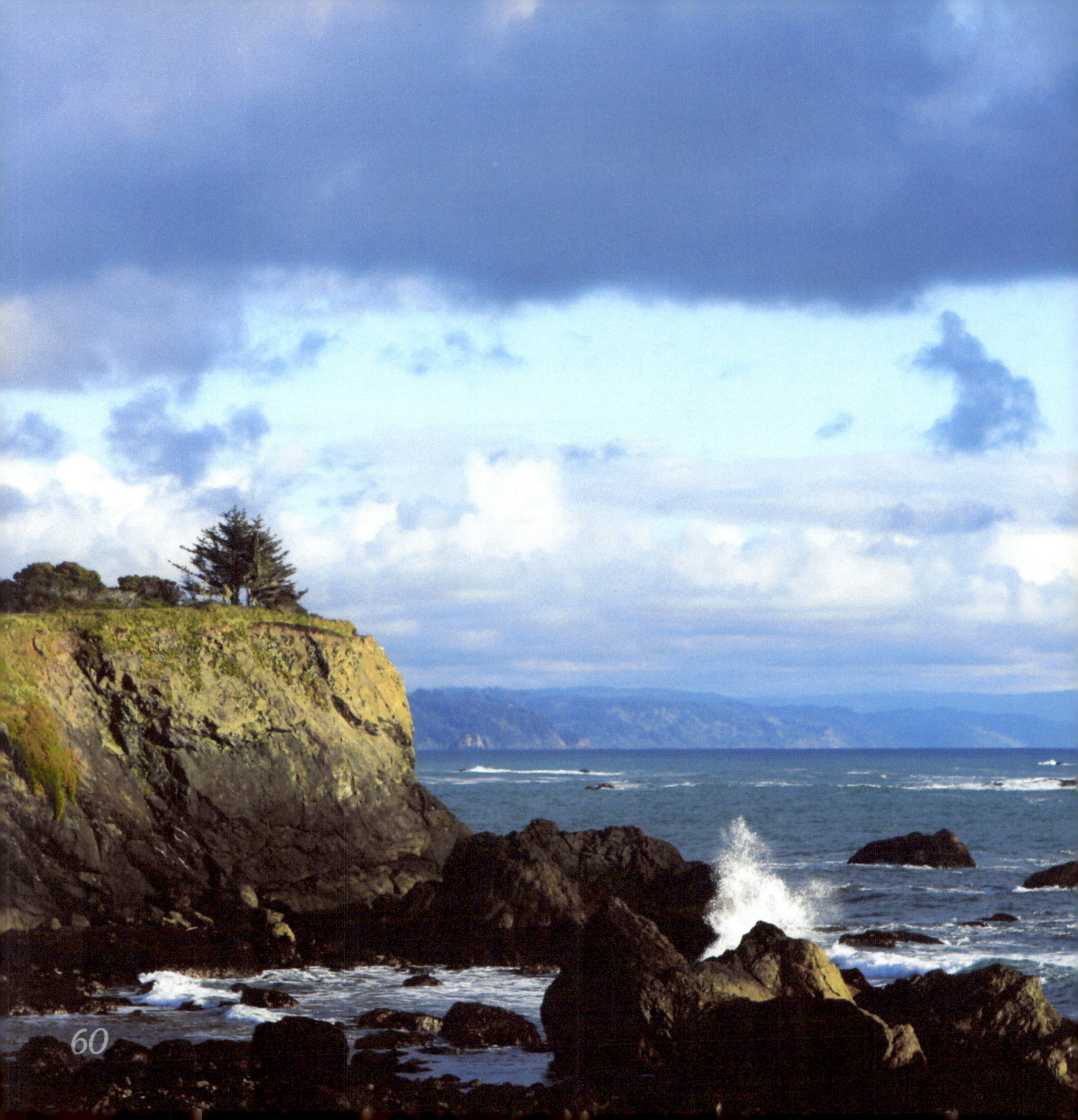

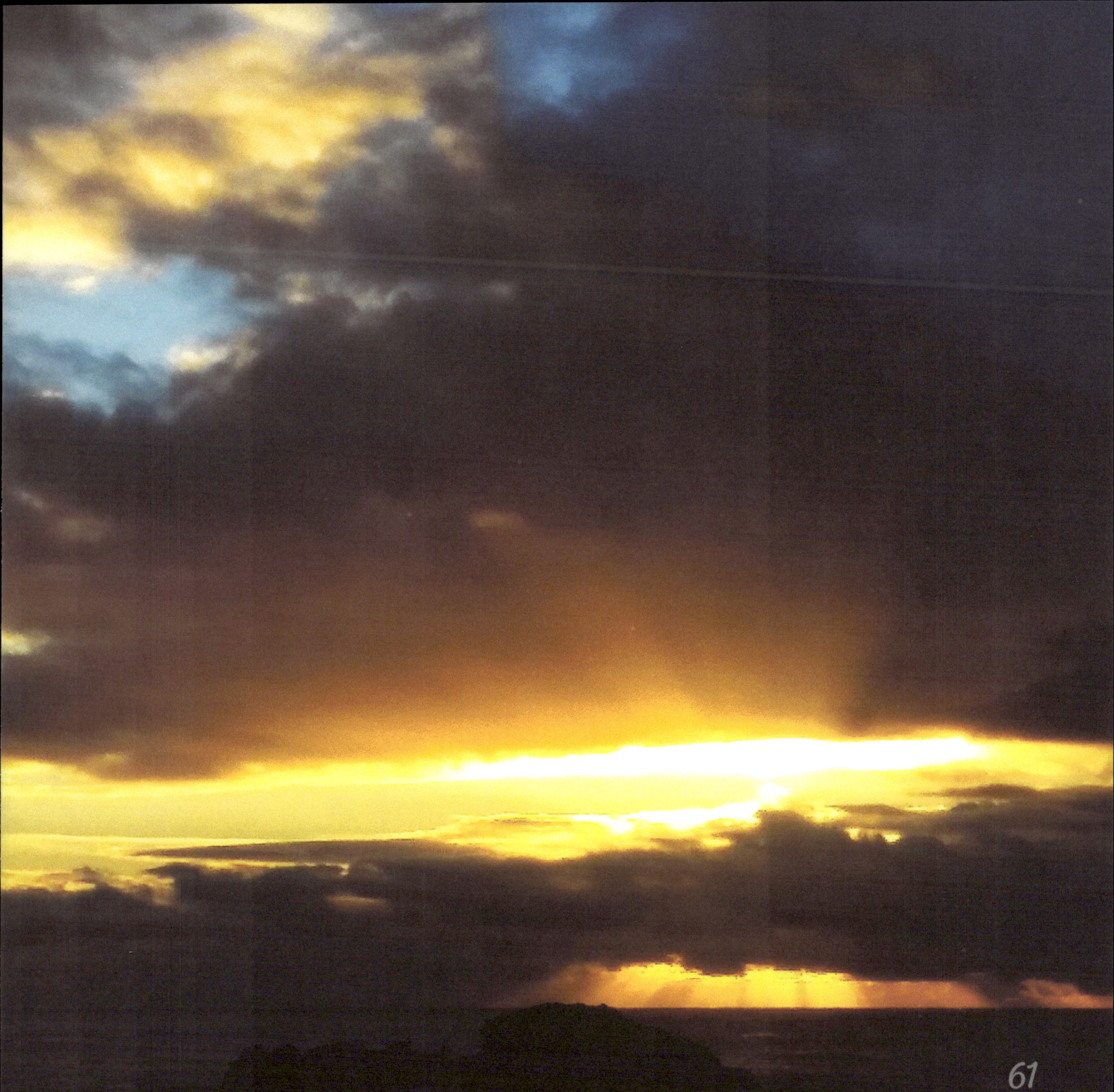

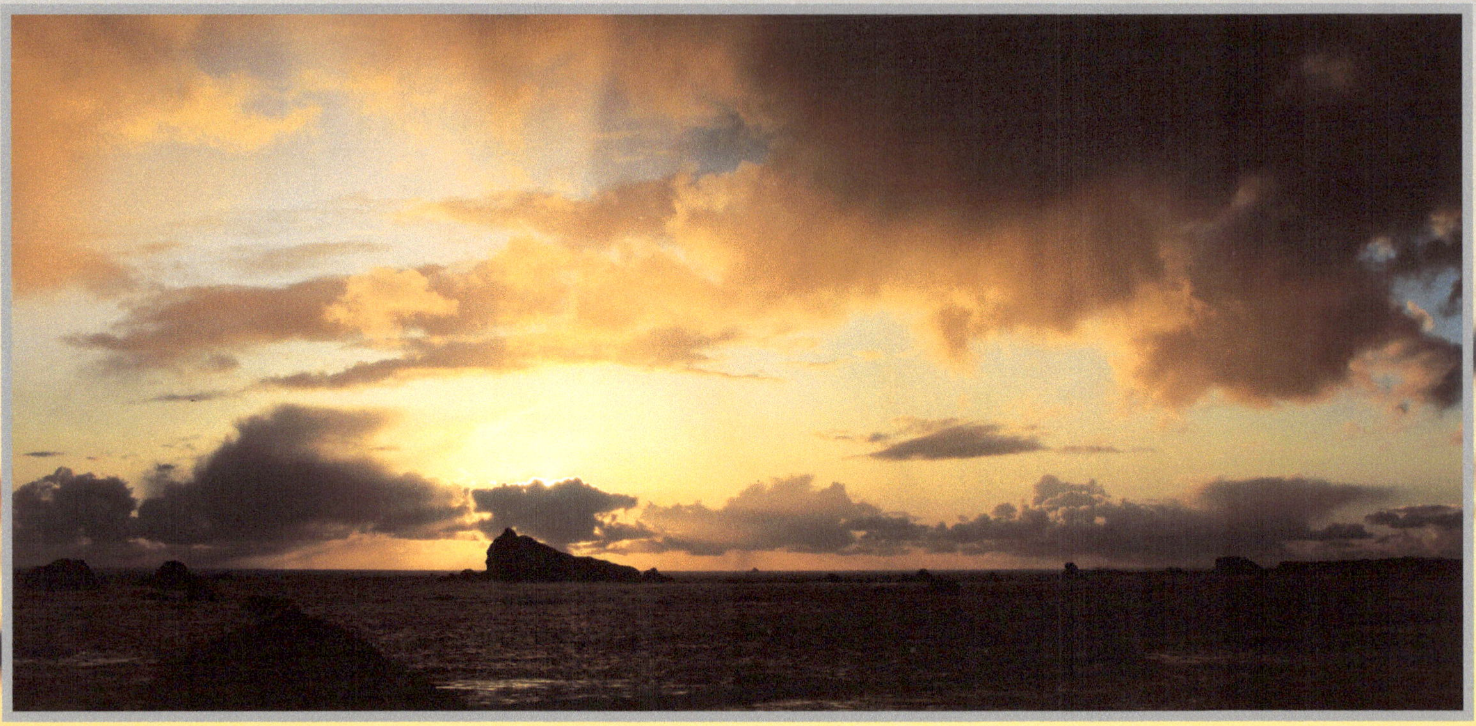

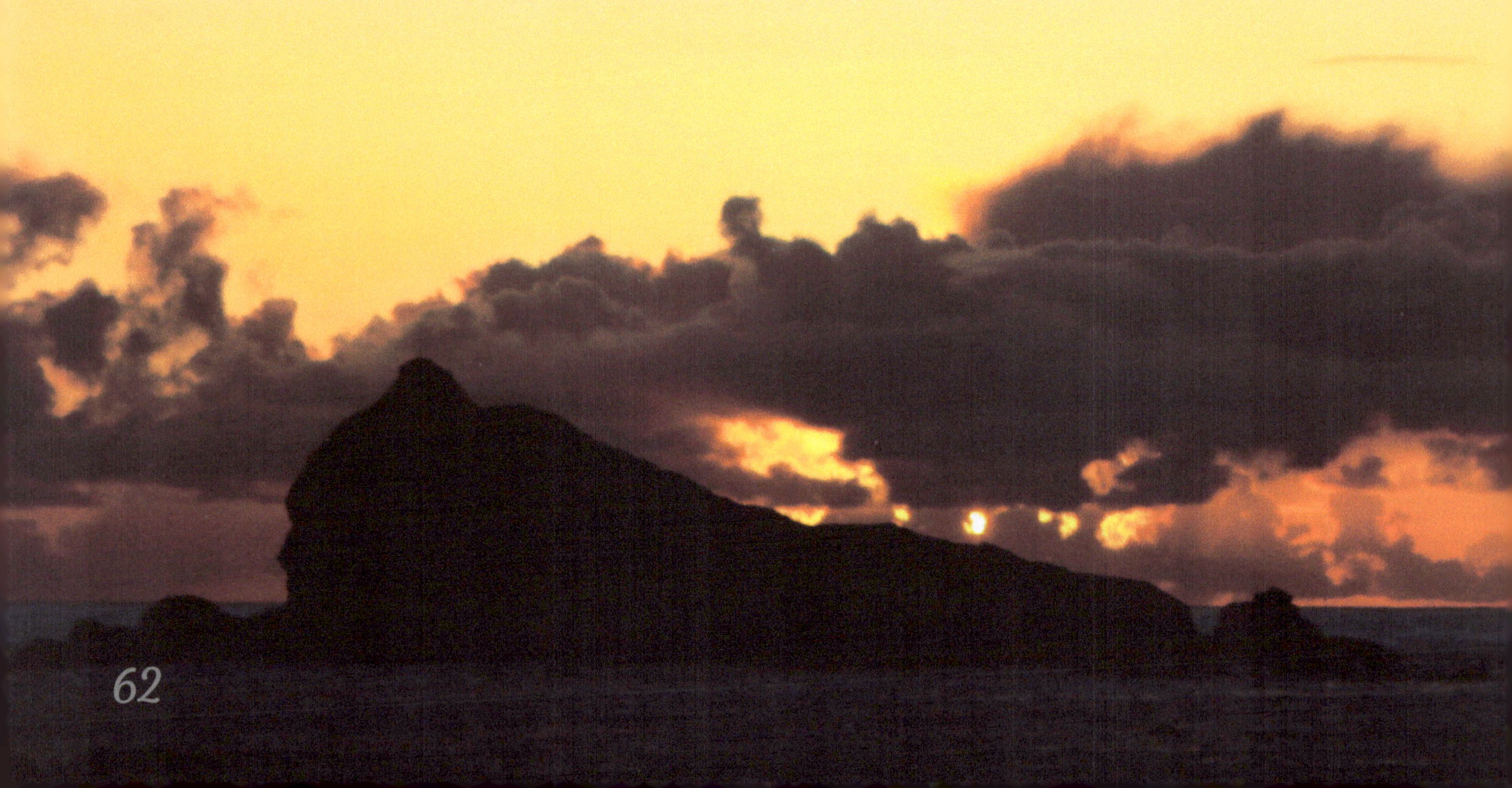

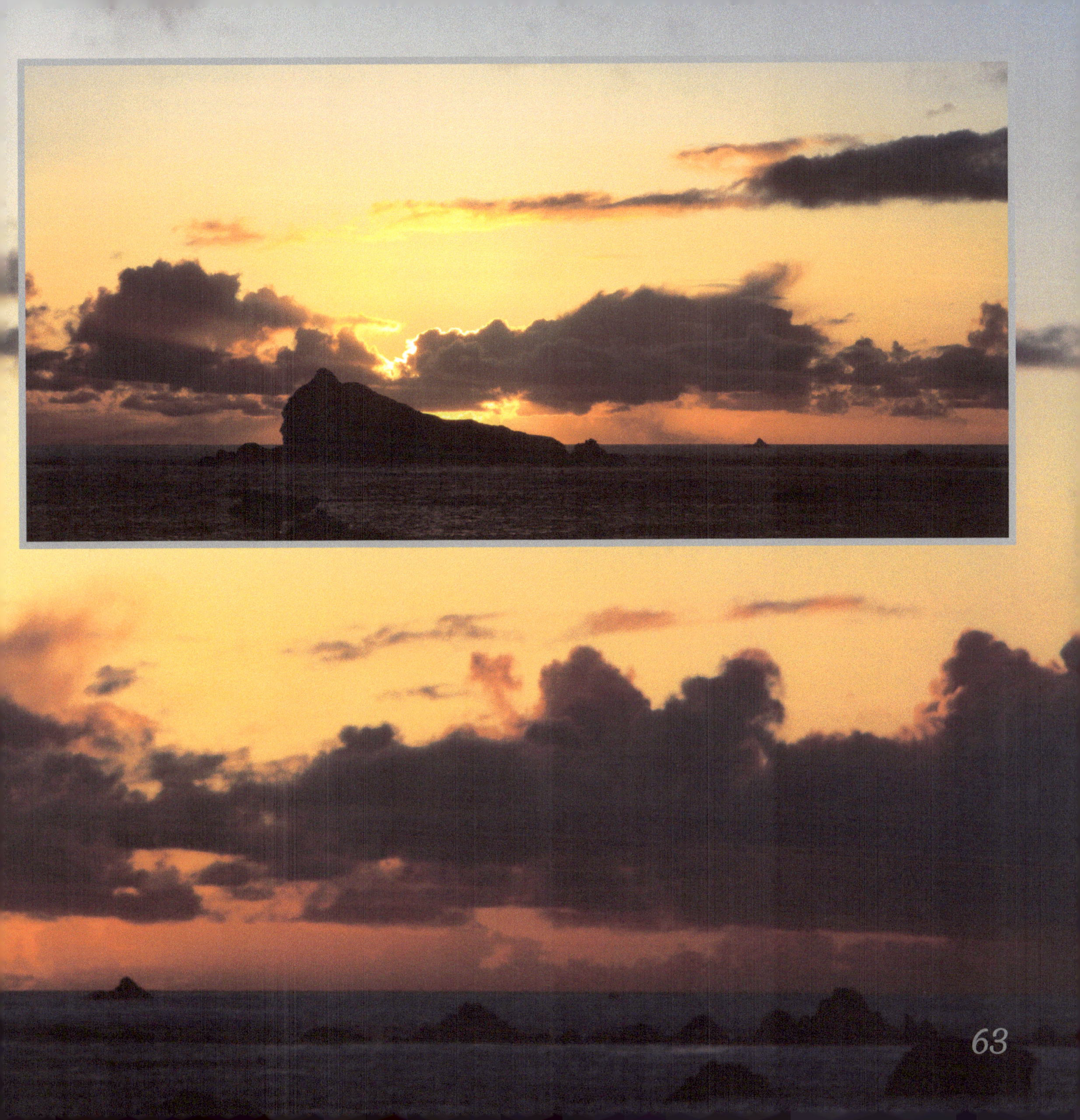

63

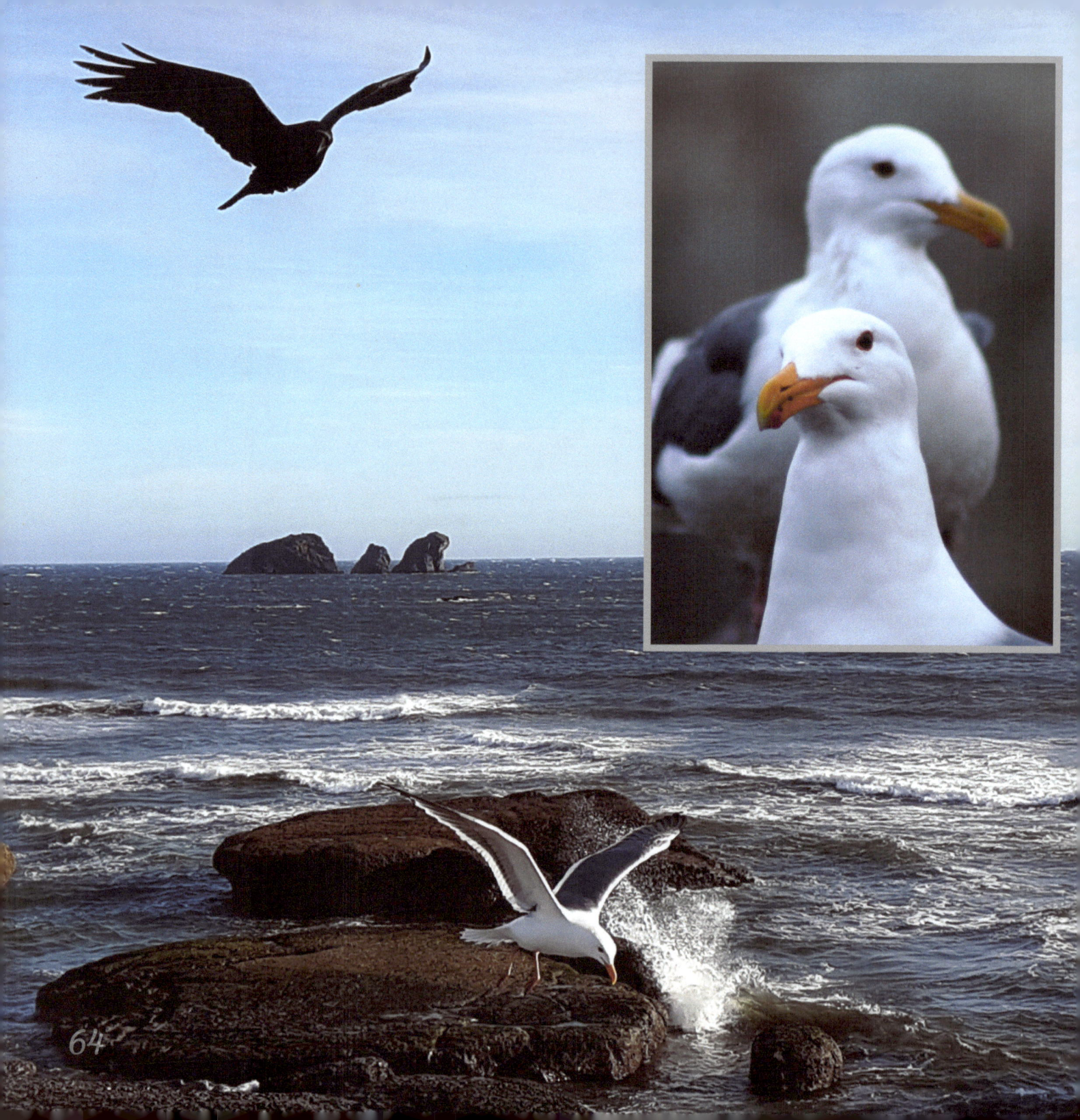

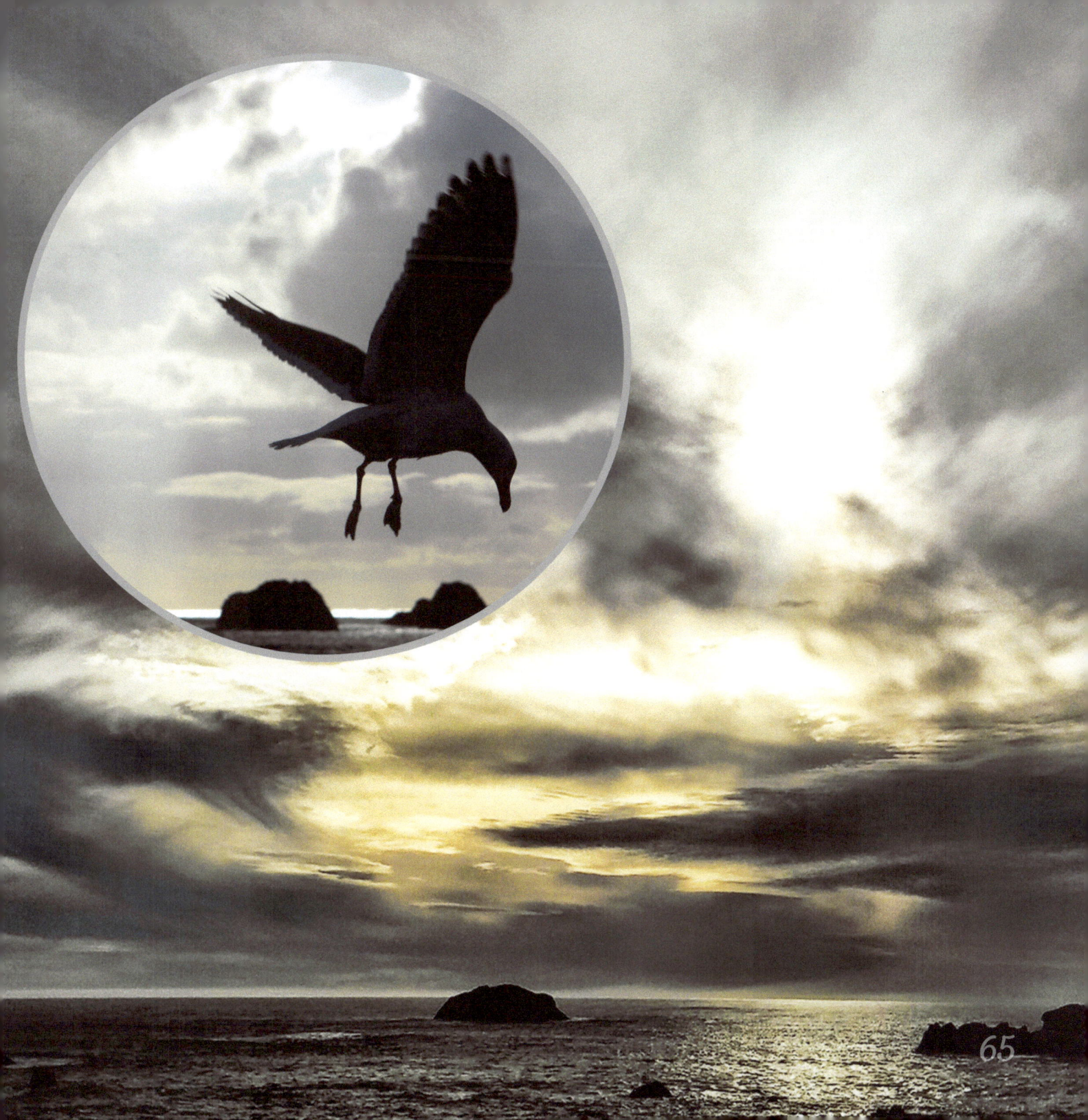

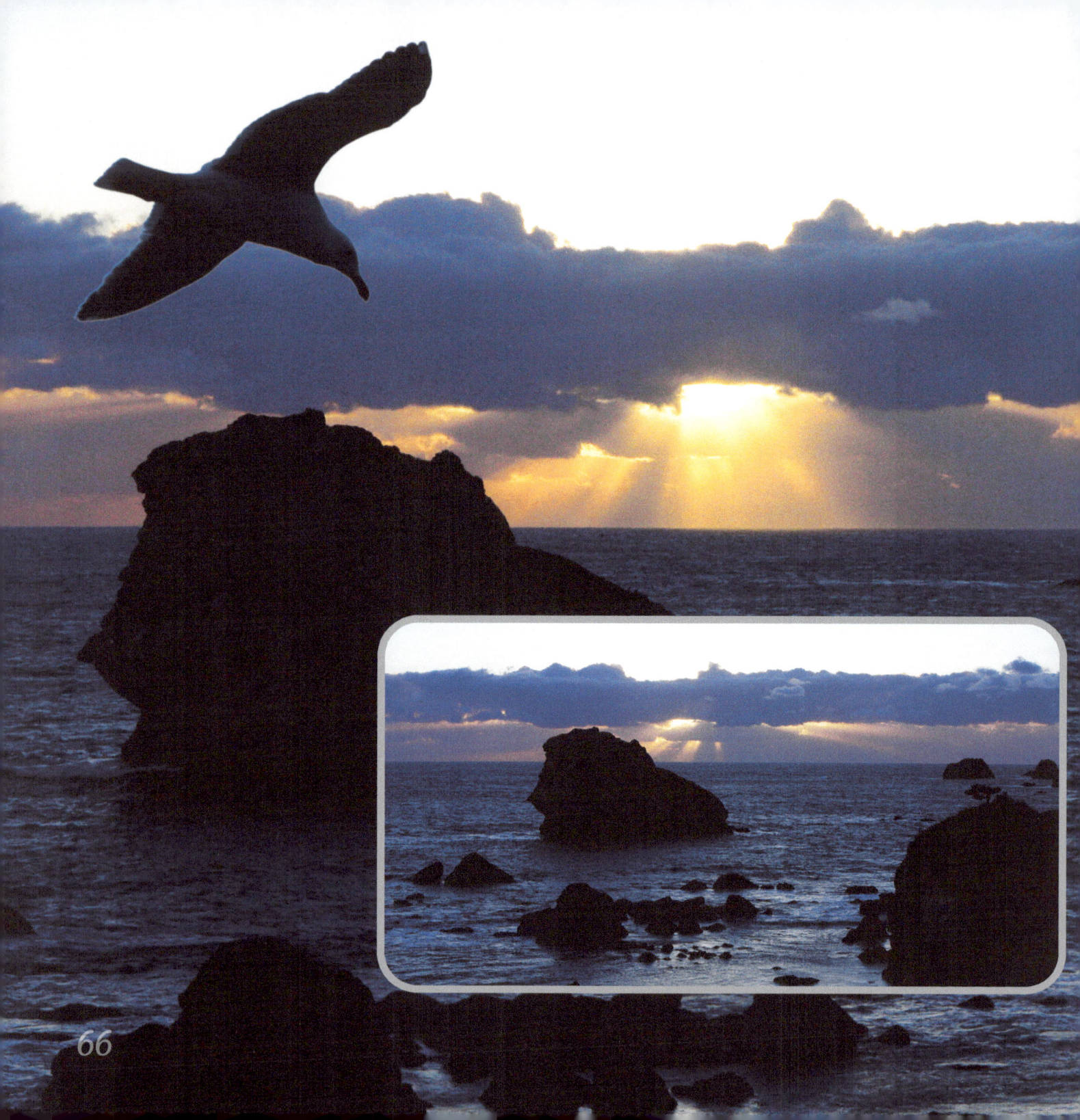

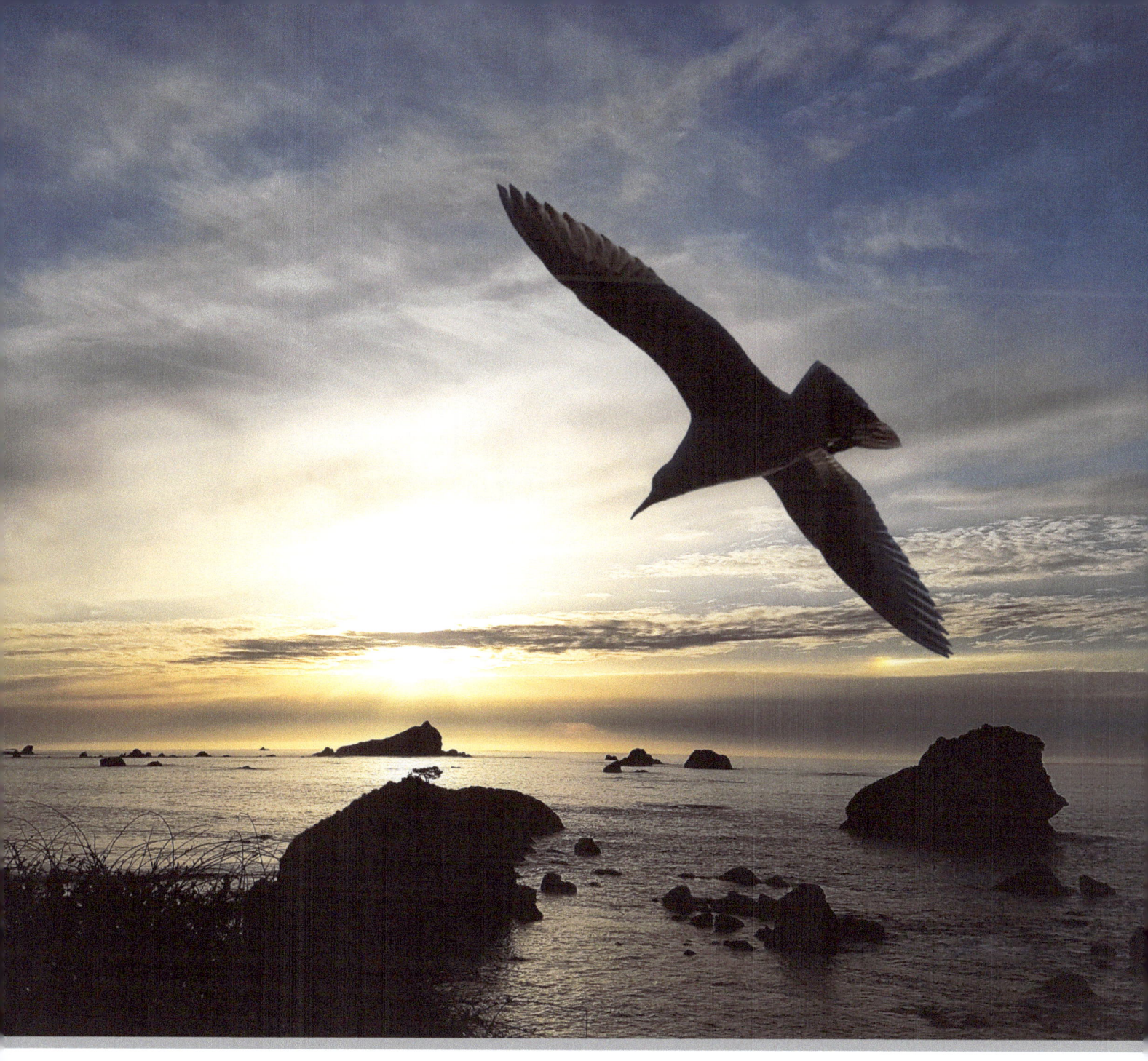

www.ingramcontent.com/pod-product-compliance
Lightning Source LLC
Chambersburg PA
CBHW051204220526
45473CB00003B/896